HERE
THERE BE
UNICORNS

Jane Yolen

HERE THERE BE UNICORNS

Illustrated by DAVID WILGUS

HARCOURT BRACE & COMPANY

San Diego   New York   London

Requests for permission to make copies
of any part of the work should be mailed to:
Permissions Department, Harcourt Brace & Company,
6277 Sea Harbor Drive, Orlando, Florida 32887-6777.

"The Lady's Garden" by Jane Yolen previously appeared in
The Magazine of Fantasy and Science Fiction, copyright © 1994 by Jane Yolen.
"The Boy Who Drew Unicorns" by Jane Yolen previously appeared
in *The Unicorn Treasury*, edited by Bruce Coville, copyright © 1987
by Jane Yolen, published by Doubleday. "Rhinoceros" by Jane Yolen
first appeared in *The Grecourt Review*, copyright © 1959 by Jane Yolen.
All reprinted by permission of the author's agent, Curtis Brown, Ltd.

Library of Congress Cataloging-in-Publication Data
Yolen, Jane.
Here there be unicorns/by Jane Yolen;
illustrated by David Wilgus.—1st ed.
p.   cm.
Summary: A collection of new and previously
published stories and poems about unicorns by Jane Yolen.
ISBN 0-15-209902-6
1. Unicorns—Juvenile fiction.   2. Children's stories,
American.   3. Unicorns—Juvenile poetry.   4. Children's poetry,
American.   [1. Unicorns—Fiction.   2. Short stories.
3. Unicorns—Poetry.   4. American poetry.]
I. Wilgus, David, ill.   II. Title.
PZ7.Y78Hk   1994
[Fic]—dc20   94-1790

Designed by Camilla Filancia
First edition   A B C D E

Printed in the United States of America

Since the unicorn

is the heraldic symbol of Scotland,

this book is dedicated to our friends there,

who have made us feel so welcome at Wayside

—J. Y.

Contents

HERE
THERE BE
UNICORNS

Two days before I wrote this poem, I watched a television show on Shakespeare's Richard II. Sir John Gielgud gave John of Gaunt's famous speech: "This royal throne of kings, this scept'red isle . . . This blessed plot, this earth, this realm, this England . . . ," which is one of my all-time favorite pieces of literature. So when I started the poem, I fell, quite naturally, into that style.

The Making of a Unicorn

"It is said of Cuvier that he could reconstruct the skeleton of a prehistoric animal from a single knucklebone."
—Odell Shepard,
The Lore of the Unicorn

Take this bone, this ivory,
This slender pyramid, this spear,
This walking stick, this cornucopia,
This twisted instrument of fear,
This mammoth tusk, this pearly thorn,
This mythic spike, this maiden's bier,
This denticle, this rib of time,
This alabaster harrow—here
We start the beast, we give it name,
That world will never be the same.

There are two really famous medieval unicorn tapestries and I have been lucky enough to see them both. The Hunt of the Unicorn was made either in 1499 or around 1515 (no one is quite sure), and it hangs in the Cloisters, a museum in New York City that was once a nunnery, brought over stone by stone from Europe. The other tapestry, The Lady with the Unicorn, was made in the early sixteenth century and is kept at the Cluny Museum in Paris, France.

Both of the tapestries (well—all of them, since each is not a single tapestry but a series, sort of like illustrations in a book without words) are known as mille-fleur tapestries, "thousand flowers," because of the backgrounds of flowering plants and bushes. Though today we mean something different when we use the word cartoon, tapestry weavers used it to mean the drawing upon which they based their work, a drawing first done in a small size on paper, then enlarged and transferred to linen with the correct colors.

This story began with those tapestries because I have loved them for as long as I can remember. I read Marriage and the Family in the Middle Ages by Frances and Joseph Gies for some background information. Another big help were the sections on embroidery and tapestry in an encyclopedia. Often I do more research for fantasy stories than I do for realistic ones! I used some of these same sources for my one unicorn novel, The Transfigured Hart.

"Unicorn Tapestry" was drafted in a single week, but that was only the beginning. There were about eight drafts that followed (two typed versions and six rounds with a heavy pen) before it was done to my satisfaction. Then I reworked it a bit more with my editor, then once again in the galleys. The problem with writing is that one is never really finished with a piece. Not even when it is printed.

Unicorn Tapestry

Princess Marian was a middle child and middle—she often complained—in everything else. Her older sister, Mildred, was beautiful and about to be married to the emperor Karlmage. Her younger sister, Margaret, was striking and about to be wed to a neighboring king, Hal. But Marian, middling pretty and middling smart and middling in all her talents, was about to be married to no one. There were simply no eligible royals left in the world.

"Or at least in the world as we know it," said her mother. She was never willing to make a completely definitive statement. She sighed and gazed fondly into Marian's eyes (not blue like Mildred's or green like Margaret's but a sort of middling muddy brown). "They are all either married, engaged, enchanted, or strayed. I am sorry, Em. There's always the convent, you know."

The tears that filled Marian's eyes were the same middling muddy color, until they slid down onto her cheeks, where they became ordinary tears. Marian wiped them away quickly. Princesses are not supposed to cry, at least not where they can be seen. She wasn't sad about the not-marrying part. It had always been her contention that marriage is not necessarily the only thing a princess can do. But she didn't want to be shut away in a convent, not when she didn't have the proper strong beliefs.

Marian left her mother's chamber and trudged slowly down the winding stone stair. She went out a little dark side door, the one that was hidden by a large tapestry. Only Marian and her sisters knew about the door. They had discovered it one day playing catch-as-who-can. The door opened onto a wild part of the vast palace gardens, near an untended lily pool.

Marian was so upset, she picked up a smooth white stone and threw it across the pond. It skipped three times before it sank. "If only stones could grant wishes," she said aloud.

"As-you-will," sang out an undistinguished brown bird on the cherry bough. For such a mud-colored bird, it had quite a lovely voice, clear yet tremulous. "As-you-will." Or at least that is what Marian thought the bird sang.

"What I will," Marian answered back, "is to be kept out of the convent. And I wish that I had something—anything—that distinguishes me. That makes me magical. Or special. Marriage is *not* necessary." She paused. "Though it could be nice."

Then she turned and walked away, feeling a fool for having made a wish upon an ordinary white skipping stone that had sunk with scarcely a ripple, and for having talked back to a totally uninteresting and ordinary bird. *Maybe*, she thought fiercely to herself, *maybe I do need to be shut away, and not necessarily in a convent, either.*

She made an angry tour around all the gardens, which took several hours. By then most of her anger had dissipated, so she slipped back past the ivy and through the hidden door.

Once in her own chamber again, Marian did what princesses always do. She worked on her embroidery. It was either that or read a book, and she had read the five leather-bound books she owned almost to shreds. New books would not be ready from the scribes until Fall, and they were sure to be boring treatises on religion or heaven or the duties of royalty. The monkish scribes had no sense of romance. What Marian really would have preferred was to have the minstrel's lays set down on strong parchment that would withstand months of rereading. As a princess, Marian knew she could command no such thing, only as a queen. And it looked as if she would never have that chance.

"Bother," she said, stitching away. This year's production was a unicorn hunt, a picture for each of the twenty dining room chairs. She was on the last one now. The year before it had been a bear hunt; the year before that, a boar.

"A bore indeed," Marian said aloud. Her sisters, being much better seamstresses, got to work on doublets and mantles for their husbands-to-be, or long stomachers for themselves. But Marian, being only middling, muddling gifted, did chairs.

The last piece was a picture of the unicorn in a golden cage, surrounded by blossoming trees, on a *mille-fleur* background. She was supposed to follow the cartoons set down by her mother's French designer. But just to make things interesting, she decided to add a tiny bird to one of the trees. "A tiny, undistinguished bird on a cherry bough," she said thoughtfully. Quickly she stitched in its outline.

"As-you-will," sang a cheery voice at her window.

When she looked up, the little brown bird was sitting on the ledge.

"Cheeky!" Marian said to the bird, but she smiled when she said it. Then she looked back to her embroidery. When she put the needle down at last, the bird flew away.

"If I were of a believing nature," she said to herself, "I would think I had *wished* that bird to me." She hesitated for a moment and stared at the patch of embroidered work. The new bit looked less like a bird than a brown lump with a yellow beak. "If I were of a believing nature," she added, "I would be happy living in a convent."

She stood and went down the stairs to dinner, where she sat, along with her sisters, her little brother (who was heir to the throne), her mother, her father, and fourteen other important folk, on the hunting-of-the-bear chairs. It was, she thought rudely, the best way to view her work.

———

The next day was one of those horrid days when the rain does not fall but simply fuzzes the air. Everything was as grey as stone and as impenetrable.

All three of the princesses sat in their mother's chamber because it had the best-drawing fire and no ceiling drips. And they talked.

They talked as their needles went in and out, in and out, and Marian talked the most. She thought that if she could only keep talking, she wouldn't feel so put out by the world, with the grey, fuzzy, impenetrable world that offered nothing to her but, possibly, lifetime tenure in a convent.

They spoke of the wars, now some twenty years in the past; they spoke of three local witches who had called up a ghost to confront a murderer at his trial; they spoke of the next-door kingdom's famous giant, who had gout; and they spoke of the coming unicorn hunt. Unicorns, being quite rare, always occasioned a special hunt. Emperor Karlmage and King Hal would both be there. The new embroidered chairs were to celebrate a successful hunt. If Marian was lucky, hunt and embroidery would be finished at the same time. She had one chair to go.

"One!" she chirruped to her sisters.

The queen's minstrel droned over his lute by the window, singing about love. He always sang about love. Or about the death of love, which seemed much the same in his mouth. Marian was thoroughly tired of the subject. She bent her head to her embroidery and saw that the lumpy brown bird had not been improved by the passage of time. She wondered if she should unpick the sorry thing and start again, then decided instead to surround it with a few more blossoms. She was working on the third flower, the color of strawberry cream, when the minstrel's string snapped.

"Bother!" Marian said aloud. The sound had caused her to jump and prick her finger so deeply it bled. The strawberry-cream blossoms got much darker because of it.

Her sisters giggled.

Hastily, the minstrel restrung his lute, but Marian had had enough. "I am going out," she said, popping the hurt finger into her mouth and sucking on it till it stopped hurting.

"It is raining," Margaret pointed out.

Marian removed the finger from her mouth. "It is *always* raining," she said. "Or at least it always rains *some*, every other day. And I am bored with sewing. And bored with love songs. I am going out."

"To do what?" asked Mildred. "You haven't finished the final chair."

That was the problem. Marian had no plans other than to leave. But she was not about to say so. "That is my secret," she said.

She wrapped herself in a good all-weather cloak and went down into the garden. As she stood by the pool, the rain-soaked air holding her close, something stirred in a nearby tree.

"As-you-will," sang a bird behind her.

She turned and stared at the cherry tree but could not see the bird. It was well hidden behind showy pink blossoms. She was certain the blossoms had not been open the day before. *And* they had been a cream color.

For a moment—only a moment—she considered the chair cover she had just been embroidering, with its blood-spattered flowers, then dismissed the connection. She was, she reminded herself, not of a believing nature. Her memory was just playing tricks.

"As-you-will," the bird sang again.

"Don't you know any other song?" Marian asked peevishly.

As if in answer, the bird trilled a song of such surpassing frills and furbelows that Marian clapped her hands in delight. The bird was *much* better than the queen's minstrel.

"Bravo!" she called to it. And at that the rain began to fall in earnest. Wrapping herself even more tightly in the cloak, Marian ran back to the castle and her mother's warm fire.

All night the rain pattered down and Marian, whose room was the highest in the tower and therefore under the roof, heard every drop. She did not sleep a wink, though her maid snored through till dawn.

As a consequence, Marian finished the final piece of embroidery, squeezed as close to the fire as she dared. It was just as well. The visiting hunters had all arrived in time for last night's dinner, and the informal, raucous meal had lasted well into the hind end of the night.

The queen's minstrel had trotted out all his hunting songs for them, though each song still had much romance and love in it: deer turning into lovely maidens, young women shot by lovers who had mistaken them for swans, and the like. Marian had left midway through a particularly long song, sent away by her mother because she had disgraced them all by yawning, and loudly.

Once in her room, Marian had discovered, much to her chagrin, that she could not sleep. Could not—or would not. It was the same. She decided to substitute embroidery for dreams. She had almost finished the thing, with stem and split stitches and couching, the face of the unicorn set in with the spiral stitch her nanny had taught her and she had never dared use before.

Much to her surprise, her unicorn really looked like a unicorn and not like a sagging deer or a deformed goat. The face, in the spiral stitch, was quite wonderful, with an almost human expression. The horn was outlined with the last of the shimmering silver thread. Only the eyes were not quite right. She couldn't think what color to make them—a deep lapis or lighter azure or perhaps the color of old gold. But when she checked her basket, there was only a muddy brown

9

thread there anyway, and she hated using it. Still, she couldn't very well go into her mother's room or her sisters', looking for thread at this hour.

And when she tucked the last of the brown stitches in, finishing off with a proper knot, she found to her surprise that she liked the brown eyes enormously. In fact she liked the whole thing: the muddy-eyed beast in its golden cage, that gold being repeated in the winking eyes of many of the flowers. She didn't have enough gold left to do a proper halter, so she left the unicorn's neck bare.

Stretching, Marian glanced out of the window. The rains had stopped and it was morning, a weak sun just rising. Everything was shimmering and fresh and green.

She suddenly remembered part of one of the minstrel's songs, something about the lawns of Eden:

> *Where the original garden thrush*
> *Syllabled all of Paradise*
> *From a hand-painted bush.*

That was what the world looked like from her window: clean and new, like the first day of the world. She took a deep breath, and that was when she heard the horn of the master of the hunt. It was a dangerous sound, sharp as a knife, cutting the clean air.

For a moment she glanced down at her embroidery and felt a keen regret for that singular beast with the spiral horn. Then, clutching the piece of cloth, she ran down the stairs. Breakfast would certainly be ready if the men were already out on the hunt.

Breakfast consisted of nightingale eggs boiled in the shell, tiny things that contrasted greatly with the goose eggs similarly cooked.

There were fresh forced-strawberries, and slabs of smoked ham—attesting to the success of the last boar hunt. There were brown breads and white breads and one kind of bread—the cook's specialty, which Marian hated—that was nearly black. She counted three different kinds of cheese, a pot of fresh-churned butter, and preserves that ranged from the bright red of raspberry to the dark plummy color of grape. For those who could not do without it, there was the traditional porridge and, to sweeten it, mashed apples. They never ate so well, even on high feast days, except at the hunt breakfast.

Marian found she was suddenly not hungry. *Perhaps*, she thought, *one needs to sleep and dream in order to feel hunger.* She set the embroidery on the table by her plate. She was all but dozing there when her sisters arrived and noisily sat on either side of her, chattering across her about the day.

Marian listened as if in a dream. They spoke of the handsome mantles their men wore, and of the jangling bells on the horses' harnesses. They commented on the emperor's fine roan stallion and the high color on the cheeks of the master of the hunt.

Suddenly Mildred pounced on the embroidery by Marian's plate. "Em!" she cried. "You've finished."

"Not quite," Margaret said. "The unicorn has no halter. You know it cannot be caught without one. Whatever were you thinking, Em?"

"I ran out of thread and it was late," Marian said, trying not to yawn.

"Let me, then," Mildred said, tucking into her pocket and fishing out a needle and three different shades of gold thread. Then, despite Marian's feeble protests, she chose the fairest of the three and proceeded to stitch in a golden rope about the beast's white neck. The stitches were small and even and, Marian had to reluctantly admit, it was the finest part of the whole piece. Still, there was something she didn't like about it.

"And those eyes!" Margaret said, taking the embroidery out of Mildred's hands. "No self-respecting magic creature has *brown* eyes, Em. Lapis—that's the thing." She dipped into her own pocket and came up with a needle, and thread the color of an early spring sky, as well as a pair of gold scissors. She unpicked the unicorn's brown right eye, quickly sewing in a lovely blue one instead.

"But I *liked* the brown eyes," Marian complained. She tugged the embroidery away from her sister. After breakfast, if she could find a match to the brown, she would try to sew that eye again.

They were still sitting at the table when the master's horn clarioned across a far glade.

"Maybe they have found the unicorn," Mildred said, two spots of color, like old bloodstains, shining on her cheeks.

"Maybe they have killed it!" Margaret added. There was a great deal of excitement in her voice.

Killed. Marian had known all along that the unicorn would be killed, not put in a cage with a yellow ribband around its neck. But somehow, with the piece of embroidery before her, like a cartoon of the actual hunt, the whole thing suddenly seemed horrible. Barbaric. She stared down at the cloth. The unicorn, with its one blue, one brown eye, stared back as if pleading for its life.

"Sister," Marian said, turning to Margaret, "lend me your scissors." She held out her hand and Margaret, without asking why, gave them to her. Quickly, Marian snipped away at the yellow threads, unpicking the gold around the unicorn's neck.

I wish, she thought, but did not say it aloud.

———

The men came back to the castle in a grim and terrible mood. Three hounds had been maimed and the horses all run to lather. The master of the hunt had taken a fall and his hunting horn, used for years by his father and father's father before him, was smashed beyond repair. The emperor had lost his best bow in a bog.

At the last minute, the unicorn had escaped. Surrounded and at bay, it had unaccountably gotten through the circle of men and horses and dogs and disappeared. The hounds could not find the scent.

"This smells of sorcery," King Hal complained.

"Witchery," added the emperor.

"Magic," said Marian's father, always the agreeable host.

Dinner that night was equally grim. No one noticed the embroidered chairs. Only Marian smiled quietly, looking down at her plate. Only Marian ate a full meal.

Halfway through the serving, there was a commotion in the entryway and suddenly, unannounced, a man entered the hall. He was not handsome, Marian thought, but he was strong limbed, with corded muscles and a beaky nose. His hair looked as if the wind might have had a hand in combing it; his clothes were well traveled and stained.

The emperor looked up from his picked-at dinner. "Malcolm!" he cried. "Cousin! We thought you were dead."

"Or vanished," added King Hal.

They stood and embraced him and brought him to meet their host.

"Have you come to be part of our hunt?" the king asked. "We could use another bow."

"Your hunt is over," Malcolm said. "But mine is just begun." He turned and smiled broadly at Marian and then at the queen. Marian wondered that she had ever thought him not handsome.

The queen nodded back. "I suspect you hunt for a wife, sir. May I commend you to my daughter Marian?"

Marian stood, furious, shaking. *This was too baldly done*, she thought. *Like a piece of meat at the market. The convent might be more to my liking.*

"A lovelier girl you could not find," her father added, which made things worse. Lovelier, indeed, when she was there between Margaret and Mildred! Marian thought to flee, like an animal chased through the woods.

But Malcolm walked to her, blocking her escape. She could not go around him without making a scene. Princesses did not make scenes. One needed to be a queen to do that.

Taking her hand, Malcolm spoke to the room at large. "There will be no marriage if only the king and queen will it," he said. "It is the lady's choice."

He looked directly at her and she noticed, with a start, that his eyes were not the same color. One was muddy brown, the other grey, almost blue. It made him look quite wild, untamed.

Marian thought about the embroidery, about the bird on the ledge, about the blossoms on the cherry bough. She thought about the un-picked golden halter and the lapis eye she'd had no time to change. She thought about the smooth white stone and her wishes.

As she was thinking still, he turned her hand over and kissed her palm. When he looked up, he whispered so that only she could hear him, "As you will, my lady. As you will."

They were married in the late Fall, the trees ablaze with color. In the middle of the ceremony, she thought rather belatedly that belief would serve as well outside the convent walls as in.

She asked for the unicorn chairs as part of her dowry.

They are in her castle still.

I was in college when I wrote the first version of this poem. I was obsessed with unicorns then as a powerful symbol. As I was frequently writing poems about love or death, this poem was at that time a perfect piece of writing, as it combined both! Plus it uses the old folk belief that a unicorn can be caught with a golden bridle.

The Death of the Unicorn

The bright-bodied hounds run silent,
The hawks have fled the sky,
For my knight lies under a bloodied shield
Near a brackish reed-whipped pond.

I seized the gold bridle from the wall
And tossed it to the pond.
It sank with a sigh, as if all earth
Sucked at the breast of an empty dream.

This story took about six weeks to write, though it should have taken me a lot less. I had the plot figured out early on. But though I wanted to get to writing it, the idea had come to me at a time when I was traveling around to conferences, giving speeches, being scintillating on panels, and all the rest of that sort of thing. So I kept putting off actually writing the story.

Still, I believe that a story gets written down when it is ready to be written down. I try never to rush things. And by my delaying the actual writing, a number of nice things happened to the story along the way. For example, the lines "His temper was as sour as his stomach . . ." and "A plague is a plague . . . whether of beauty or terror." They crept in late, and I like them both.

My Latin teacher in high school used to say "Tibi licet" ("It is allowed") when we asked permission during class to go off to the bathroom. I have always wanted to use that—or its opposite, "Non licet"—in a story. For the rest of the Latin I had to ask my friend John Crowley for help. He went to a Catholic high school where Latin was a major subject and not, like at mine, a two-year option.

The canonical hours, when monks at a monastery or abbey would pray, are matins (with lauds), prime, tierce, sext, nones, vespers, and compline. That sounds like a poem. Other bits and pieces about medieval monasteries I gleaned from Ellis Peters's wonderful mystery novels about the Middle Ages, starring that detective extraordinaire, Brother Cadfael.

An Infestation of Unicorns

In the apple orchard behind the great stone walls of Cranford Abbey there were five varieties of apple tree. Three bore red apples, rosy and round. One bore apples the color of fine old wine. And one bore apples that were, in their prime, a startling gold. Not the gold of the sun or the gold of a coin, but rather a color that would put mustard to shame and make wheat weep, if such were possible.

It was on these golden apples that the unicorns dined annually when they came through Cranford on their great migration.

For years no one had disturbed the unicorns at their feast. Singly and alone a unicorn is a magnificent animal. But in a herd they can prove exceeding dangerous, especially if disturbed while eating. And especially if disturbed while eating *golden* apples.

But when a certain Father Aelian became abbot of the abbey, having come from another abbey in another kingdom altogether, he brought with him a receipt for apple cider that had been in his family for generations. The receipt called for golden apples and it was hoped that the sale of this cider would help restore Cranford Abbey and its coffers to their former glory, for the place had fallen upon bad times.

So the battle lines were drawn in the Autumn, when apples are at their ripest—monks against unicorns. It was a rather uneven contest, for the monks thought that to harm a unicorn brought about the greatest of misfortunes.

The unicorns had no such thoughts about monks.

At the end of that first Fall, the tally stood like this: One monk, Brother Aelford, pierced through the hand. One priest, Father Alwain, run through at the thigh. Two novitiates with turned ankles from scampering away, and one with a skinned knee from falling down *while* scampering away. Three infant oblates—those young boys whose parents pledge them to God and thus to an abbey—awaking each night with screaming nightmares.

The unicorns were untouched.

And the apples? All gone, devoured as usual by the unicorn herd.

In the town of Cranford the people began to make jokes about the abbot's war. "To fight an apple-bapple" meant "to wage an uneven contest." "As rare as a golden apple in the Lord Abbot's garden" was how the Cranforders described something that did not exist at all.

The children of Cranford took to reciting nasty rhymes while bouncing balls on the Cranford cobbles, rhymes such as:

> *See the monks all in a row;*
> *In come the unicorns . . . down they go.*

And little girls playing skip-rope were heard to say, in a singsong manner:

> *Abbot, Abbot, say your prayers,*
> *I hear a unicorn on the stairs.*

Soon even Abbot Aelian heard of these japes. He was not amused. He felt that the entire countryside was laughing at the monastery, at the monks and—most particularly—at him. And he was right. Now, the good abbot was not a man upon whom laughter sat with any ease. This had something to do with the deep creases on his forehead from frowning all the time. His old nurse had remarked that he had been born that way. Well, actually, she had said, "Born with a forehead creased and no funny bone at all, poor mite." It was true. He was a good man, but he had no sense of humor.

So the second Fall, Abbot Aelian set his monks to guard the garden, the priests and older brothers at each gate, the novitiates at the foot of the trees, the infant oblates high in the branches as lookouts. Aelian directed the battle like a good general, from the safety of the heavy stone monastery walls. But the only arms he allowed his soldiers were pitchforks for protection and toweling to snap at the beasts. The boys in the trees had buckets of warm water to cast down on the unicorns.

That Fall's battle was, if anything, worse than the first. Unicorns are wily animals. It says so, right in the bestiaries. They can leap any sort of fence, they can avoid any sort of trap, they care about neither pitchforks nor toweling, and they positively love water. They can only be captured, as everyone knows, by a pure maiden with a golden halter. And a maiden—as any fool could tell you—is the one thing not allowed within a monastery. Or in the garden behind.

So this time, after the migration was past and the six monks, one priest, and four novitiates who had been injured were back on their feet, and after the three infant oblates with screaming nightmares had been sent home to their mothers for cosseting, the good abbot made up a petition that he caused to be tacked up on walls all about the countryside. The petition read, in part:

WANTED: HEROES
Fight a Beast, Win a Prize:
Bragging Rights in
Three Kingdoms
And a Share in the Cider Profits

Heroes flocked to the door all that winter, for such is the lure of money, even money that has not been made yet, nor counted. And actually, future money often seems the greater.

"Apple Eaters" was the name the Cranford townsfolk gave these heroes.

The heroes came in all shapes and sizes, mostly big.

There was the overlarge Sir Geoffrey of Stonewait Manor, a giant of a man who sat a horse with feet the size of dinner plates.

There was the very large Sir Humphrey Hippomus of Castle Dire, whose horse had feet like soup tureens.

There was the extra-large Sir Sullivan Gallivant of the Long Barrow

Gallivants, who was too big for any horse and so rode in a tumbrel pulled by matched bays.

And a hundred other heroes besides.

They spoke languages as diverse as Aramaic, Pictish, and Greek. They wore armor or togas or tartans or albs. Some preferred swords, some preferred slings, or bows, spears, or pikes. Some—like Sir Sullivan—even smoked and so looked like dragons on a bad day.

The abbot greeted each and every one and gave each and every one a dinner that further depleted the abbey's stores. He listened to their pedigrees and their stories of mighty deeds. He listened to their plans.

Every one of them said that for a single unicorn, a sword or sling or bow or spear or pike *could* suffice. But for a large and migrating herd of unicorns the only sure thing was a pure maiden—possibly several, if they could be found—to be used as a lure.

And that, of course, was the one thing the abbot could not allow.

"No women," he said. "And no girls. It's the rule."

"Then—no golden apples," the heroes all agreed, though usually after the dinner, wiping their large mouths on Abbot Aelian's fine damask table linen. And as the heroes left, by ones and twos and threes, they trampled the grass all around. In their own way they were as bad as the unicorns.

Now our story turns to one of the infant oblates, a boy named James (his mother called him Jamie, but that was before his stepfather had given him to the Church, which does not believe in nicknames).

James marched, slightly timidly, up to the abbot's door.

"Come," called the abbot, a command, not an invitation.

"Lord Abbot," James said, his face reddening, then paling with the effort of speaking to the abbot, "perhaps I can be of some help."

"Nonsense, child," the abbot said. Then, seeing James's blanched face, he added—for he was not an unfeeling man—"No one can help. Not even the heroes. God is trying us." He looked years older than when he had arrived at the abbey just eighteen months earlier. His temper was as sour as his stomach these days, but he would not take it out on the boys.

"There is one hero who has not yet come," James said.

"And who is that?" Abbot Aelian asked. "I am sure I have given dinner to every hero within the seven kingdoms around."

"A small hero, but a hero nonetheless."

"A small hero," the abbot mused, "would not eat much."

"In my stepfather's lands there is a hero named . . . Sandy." James's face got red again.

"An odd name for a hero," remarked the abbot, suspiciously.

"And a very . . . odd . . . hero," agreed James. "I could write Sandy . . . and ask for help."

"Nonsense, child, I will write."

"Sandy won't come if *you* write. Begging your pardon, sir. But Sandy is . . . is . . . very particular," James said.

"Too *particular* to answer an abbot?" asked Abbot Aelian. He rubbed a long, elegant finger aside his nose. "This Sandy wouldn't be of a devilish nature? We cannot have that, you know."

"Oh, no, sir," James said. He switched back and forth from one foot to the other. "Not devilish at all. But . . . but different."

"I am not sure," Abbot Aelian said, and waved James out the door.

But a week later, after having gone over the abbey's accounts one last time, he summoned the boy to him. "I am still not sure," he said. "But there is nothing left to do. Write to this . . . this . . . hero, Sandy."

So James composed a letter, full of inkblots because he didn't have his calligraphy quite perfect yet. The letter read:

Dear Sandy—
We need help on account of the unicorns. Can you be a hero again?
The abbey needs you.
    Brother James
P.S. Abbot Alien says no girls.

The abbot read it over and said, only mildly scolding, "You have misspelled my name, but it is a difficult name at that. You are not a brother yet, not even a novitiate, but never mind. There are already enough blots on the page." And he sent the letter on.

Now, James did not come from too far away, but far enough so that it took the letter nearly a month to arrive, and that at the hind end of Winter. And it took the hero Sandy nearly a month more to prepare, which brings us to the fore end of Spring. And then Sandy was almost three months on the road, with side jaunts to rescue two and a half maidens in danger. (The half was not really in danger, only having an argument with her husband-to-be. Sandy counseled putting off the wedding and the half maiden suggested marrying Sandy instead. That was when Sandy suddenly discovered a dragon nearby that needed dispatching.)

So it was not until Summer's blush was on the trees that James's hero, Sandy, entered the courtyard of Cranford Abbey.

James greeted the hero as if he had been waiting with less patience than an infant oblate ought. And so he had, watching out of the window slits every day when he should have been hard at his lessons. His Latin had suffered for it, likewise his Greek. And he hadn't improved his calligraphy one whit all Winter. It was still full of unsightly blots.

But when he saw the great white horse with its barrel chest and

24

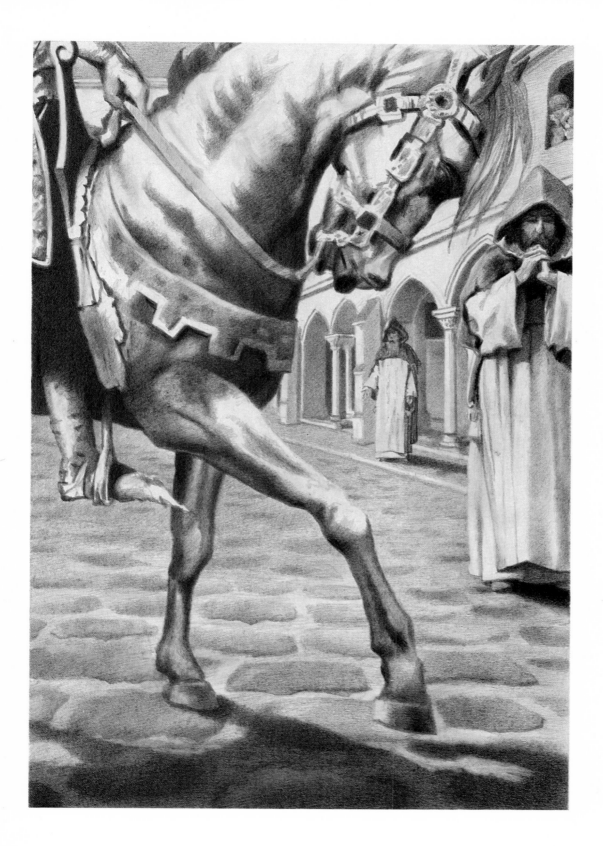

broad feet and the forelock plaited with a red ribband, he ran from the escritorium, shouting, "Sandy! Sandy!"

"Hush, brother," came the hero's voice, a remarkable tenor more suited to a bard than a fighting man. "I came as soon as I could."

Then James, forgetting he was supposed to be learning to be a monk, ran into the hero's arms.

"There, there, Brother James," Sandy said, scrubbing the boy's as yet untonsured head with unrelenting knuckles. "There, there. I have missed you, too."

At that moment, Abbot Aelian appeared and the two—boy and hero—sprang apart.

"Sir," Sandy said, executing a remarkably fluid half bow for some- one in armor, "I have come to do you service." The armor was bur- nished a bit brightly from dragon's fire, and dented in odd places, clearly from battles.

"Well, well . . ." was all the abbot said.

"You wanted a hero," James said, "and Sandy is the best—the very best—in our dukedom."

"If you give me leave," Sandy said, "I will rid you of this infestation of unicorns. A plague is a plague, my Lord Abbot, whether of beauty or terror, don't you agree?"

"I take your meaning, Sir Knight," the abbot said. "Will you have dinner with us tonight?"

"No, my lord. I will stay in my encampment beyond the garden walls till the deed is done," said Sandy. "That is how I work. Apart and alone." Another bow, as delicately sketched as the first, and Sandy remounted the white horse.

"Can I camp with Sandy?" asked James.

"*Non licet*," the abbot said disapprovingly, which is Latin for "No."

"May James be my messenger?" Sandy asked.

"*Certes*," said the abbot, which is Latin for "Yes."

"*Gratias domine*," Sandy replied, the Latin for "Thanks, Abbot."

If the abbot was surprised that the hero knew Latin, a language not normally known by knights, he made no mention of it. In those days, Latin was normally reserved for monks, well-bred ladies, and scholars, mostly of the religious kind. Heroes knew the Latin words for armor parts, body parts, and horse maneuvers. But not much more. Still, it had been a long Winter of dinners with heroes for the abbot, so he merely smiled.

Thus it was that the hero Sandy stayed just outside the orchard, though each day was spent setting up a series of interesting high wooden pens and gates, like a maze. James helped festoon the palings with bright golden ribbands till it looked ready for some kind of fest. They worked past the blossom season and well into the season of fruit, when the apples grew from small buttons into well-rounded globes.

Each day, right at noon, Abbot Aelian came down to check the hero's progress, and each time he asked, "Will you have dinner with me this night?"

And each day, Sandy replied, "*Non licet.* I stay apart and alone."

James struggled down twice daily, once after prime and again after tierce, with a large basket filled with food from the monks' own larder. He picnicked with his hero, then went back to work at his alphas and omegas, at his fine monastic hand. He was so happy to be with Sandy again, he was able to catch up on his studies and even passed the other boys. The abbot was well pleased, though he never said a word to either James or Sandy about it.

And then, of a sudden, it was Fall, the apples fairly bursting off the boughs. The first thunder of hoofbeats was heard, like a distant storm.

"The unicorns, fair knight . . . " the abbot began.

"I have heard them these three nights running," said Sandy.

"Because you are a hero?" asked James.

"Because I have been sleeping on the ground, and you on a cot in the *dortoir*, little brother," Sandy said, smiling.

"What will you need from me?" Abbot Aelian asked.

"Only that you keep the monks and priests indoors. And especially the novitiates and the infant oblates," said Sandy. "A hero's business can be . . . complicated . . . by small boys." A swift but compelling hero smile lit Sandy's face. "Oh, yes, and shutter all the windows."

"*Intellego omnes,*" the abbot said, which is Latin for "I understand all."

"Perhaps you do," Sandy replied. "Perhaps you do."

The abbot took James by the hand, something he had never done before, and led him into the monastery. Aelian never looked back, but James did, longingly, fearfully, his worry writ large in his eyes and on his mouth.

Sandy waved to him and then, when the abbot disappeared through the heavy doors and James was almost pulled through, Sandy blew the boy a kiss.

James smiled and—suddenly—all the fear was gone from his face.

The unicorn herd arrived before dawn, at the canonical hour of prime, a parade of silver hooves and silver manes and spiraling horns. They pranced and they paced, they did pirouettes and caprioles, heels kicking in the air. The lead stallion spun around in place three times and was followed at a slower pace by the other males. Then the females beat their perfect feet on the ground, marking the soil with prints as clear as brands.

Sandy stood in the center of the orchard, spear raised, waiting.

When the great stallion cried out in that peculiar voice unicorns have, somewhere between the whinny of a horse and the blat of a deer, Sandy answered back. It was both an echo and a challenge.

The head of the herd rose up on his hind legs and sniffed the air.

Sandy called out again, this time in that high tenor voice, singing:

Thread the maze,
Find the maid,
Seek the hero
Unafraid.

When the last note of the song ended, the unicorns lifted their heads. Then, suddenly, they leaped up over the stone walls, so high their hooves never touched a single rock. Cavorting and capering, they began to thread the wooden maze. The wind blew the golden ribbands out so that they flapped like banners in the air.

The maze was drawn with rowan boughs and the yellow ribbands had been blessed with holy oil, but it was the song that led the unicorns through the maze, head to tail to head to tail, as though they were tamed. As if enchanted—and perhaps they were—the unicorns did not stop to graze on grass or nibble the ripened apples on the boughs. They did not stop to nuzzle the windfalls, neither the gold ones nor the reds. Instead they crowded toward the center court and waited while their leader, the great stallion, marched up to the hero.

And there Sandy stood, back against a tree so laden with yellow apples they draped the hero like a golden robe.

The stallion pointed his horn at Sandy's breast but did not thrust forward. Nor did Sandy pierce him with the spear. Instead, unicorn and hero gave twin sighs and sank down together in front of the tree.

Then, gently, quietly, Sandy removed a yellow ribband from the

29

spear and tied it, halterlike, over the stallion's nose and under his chin, and carefully pulled his white forelock through, quickly braiding it in a lover's knot. The stallion's eyes, the color of antique gold, closed, and Sandy began to sing again, so quietly that only the two of them could hear the words.

When the song was done, Sandy pushed the great beast's heavy head away and stood, pulling the unicorn up by the halter. Together, beast and hero walked companionably back through the maze, the herd coming docilely behind.

They walked down the road till they were lost in the bright sunlight, till those who watched through the window slits thought they had disappeared into heaven itself.

But James knew differently.

And so did the abbot.

"Your hero left a white horse," the abbot said.

"Yes," James said, his face a map of misery. "Its name is Carrywell."

"A good name for a horse," the abbot said.

"Yes," James answered, his lower lip trembling. "And a good horse, too."

"I think the horse needs to go home," the abbot said. "Can you manage, do you think?"

"Oh, yes," James said, his face daring to show some hope.

"Word came three days ago that your stepfather has died. You are the duke now, my boy. Your mother needs you."

James's face was suddenly wreathed in smiles.

"And so, I think, does your sister. When you see her, give her my thanks," Abbot Aelian said.

"My . . . sister?" James asked carefully.

"The hero," Abbot Aelian said. "Sandy. She will need her horse—and her brother—when she gets home with that herd." He smiled, and it made his face look years younger.

James took a deep breath and let it out slowly. "*Certes*," he said. And smiled back.

I had been at our Scottish house for four weeks without writing anything, which is, for me, practically a lifetime. I usually write every day. I had had the flu, a particularly vicious stomach virus, which had put me further behind. And then one morning, I took out my unicorn folder and began reading some of the material I had collected on early unicorn myths. It prodded me into not one but two stories, "De Natura Unicorni" and this one.

Of course, part of what fed this story are the marvelous mille-fleur tapestries of the unicorn in the garden I had seen in Cluny some thirty years earlier, the panels set apart by long, spiral narwhale horns. But I didn't make the connection to this story until days after writing it.

The Lady in this story is clearly a White Goddess figure. The three unicorns might be some sort of reference to the Trinity, though I doubt it. Wishart is named after the Protestant martyr George Wishart, who was burned at the stake about a ten-minute walk from our Scottish home. And Waverly, despite what the unicorns believe, was named after the hero in Sir Walter Scott's famous novel Waverley (different spelling), which was sitting on my desk as I worked on this tale. It is no wonder this story has a very British feel to it.

As to why there are apples in this story and the last—a question my editor asked me—apples are mentioned specifically in unicorn lore as being something unicorns love to eat. And as there was an apple tree in the Garden of Eden, I could not resist giving the Lady's garden ("there from the beginning of things") that very tree.

The Lady's Garden

In the Lady's garden lived three unicorns. They were all old—Lady, garden, and unicorns—having been there from the beginning of things. The garden was kept from the sight of the World by a very large stone wall that was overgrown with spindly weeds and thistles, and hairy moss plugging up the chinks.

When the sun shone down, the unicorns liked to lie under the apple tree, which was the oldest thing of all in the garden. Its branches hung to the ground, gnarled and misshapen but covered with the most delicious red apples the year round.

When it rained, which was for an hour every other day and twice on Tuesdays, regular as clockwork, the unicorns would stay in the stone barn, snugged together in the sweet-smelling hay. The patter on the barn roof then took on a soporific rhythm, and often the unicorns would doze and dream. Their dreams were always about running over great green swards, the wind through their white manes. Always.

If the Lady dreamed—or even if she napped—no one knew for sure, for she spoke only of waking things: tide and sun and wind and rain and the changing of seasons.

On one side of the garden was, as I have said, the World. On the other was the great Ocean. It was the Ocean's tides that were often the subject of the Lady's discourse. And though she may have thought any trouble to the garden would come to it from the World's side, it was the Ocean that did, in the end, bring about her direst time.

Now, though the unicorns were all terribly old, they were not the same age. The oldest was Wishart, whose skin was almost translucent; it was a kind of pearly white, like the inside of certain shells. When he walked—and he never ran—he moved with an ancient grace. His breath smelled musty, like a bowl of crushed flower petals. He rarely listened to anything but the sound of the Ocean outside the wall.

The second oldest was Tartary. Her skin was like vellum and looked brittle but wasn't. In fact it was as soft as an infant's and smelled that sweet-sour infant smell, as if talc and sour milk had been mixed together. Tartary listened only to the Lady's voice.

The third oldest—they called her Infanta, when they called her anything at all—still had a bit of spirit to her walk and a bit of flint in her amber eyes. Even her horn was still the gold of new-minted coins, while the other unicorns had horns more like the color of the full moon.

If Wishart listened only to the sound of the Ocean, and Tartary listened only to the Lady, Infanta heard the sounds of the Earth growing: grass and leaves and timothy in the fields. She could distinguish between oak and ash on the rise, though the sound of rowan growing made her tremble all over.

And the Lady? She was old but she never seemed to age. Except her eyes, which had once been the deep, rich blue of a Spring sky, were now faded like the skies over Winter.

Now, the way that trouble came to the garden was this. It was a small thing, but the Lady should have known that small things carry the greatest dangers. Didn't a tiny viper bite the heel of a hero and bring him low? Didn't ants tunnel through the great walls of Cathay and grind whole sections to dust?

For the first time in years—in centuries, actually—there was a strange sound outside one of the gates in the wall. Those gates, normally so overgrown with bramble hedge and briar on the World's side and so besieged by the Ocean on the other, needed no guards or wards. In fact, the Lady and the unicorns scarcely remembered from one year to the next that the gates existed. But this one lambent Spring day, right after the hour's rain, there was something rather like the wailing of a discontented child by the northeastern gate. No, *exactly* like the wailing of a discontented child. The wailing went on from the moment the rain ended until quite past teatime, or about three hours. At that point, Infanta stomped three times with her left forefoot and shook her head until the white mane flew about as light as milkweed silk.

"What *is* that noise?" she asked.

Neither Tartary—who listened only to the Lady—nor Wishart—who listened only to the sea—bothered to answer. But Infanta continued anyway. "It is louder than grass growing. Louder than a gully full of Queen Anne's lace and campion. Louder even than the bursting open of marigolds, which is very loud indeed." And she went to complain directly to the Lady, who had heard the sound already.

"If I didn't know any better," said the Lady, "I would say it is a child—and a very young child at that—lying in a reed basket washed up on the Ocean's small shingle." And because the Lady was blessed with a certain amount of prescience, which is another way of saying she could see a bit into the future, Infanta knew exactly what they would find.

The Lady sent one of her most trusted winds to leap over the wall and report back. It was a very small wind, hardly more than a breeze, really. When it returned, it reported in a voice made sweet with baby's breath and tart with brine, "It is a very young child lying in a basket."

"A reed basket," the Lady said, a great deal of satisfaction in her voice.

"Well, nettles and linen, actually," the breeze answered. Breezes, for all they are lightweight, insist on being factual. It is the habit of preachers and politicians as well.

The Lady made a face at the breeze. She hated being caught in a mistake. But then she smiled at the breeze because it had, after all, merely been reporting, not making judgments. And then the Lady instructed slightly larger breezes to waft their gauzy shifts together into a rope to hook through the handles of the basket. In this

35

way the child was raised up and over the wall and into the garden proper.

And that, you see, was the Beginning of the End.

The child was a boy. That was evident at once. And he was hungry. That, too, was evident. But whose child he was or why he was there at all, those questions could not be answered, not even by the Lady. Indeed those questions were *never* to be answered, but by teatime the next day it didn't matter because by then they were all thoroughly besotted with him.

Infanta was the first to fall under his spell, when he raised his little hand up to her mane and tangled his chubby fingers in it.

The next to fall was Tartary. "He has," she cooed to the Lady, "your voice." By which she meant she was listening to him, though not really hearing him; for certainly the baby did not have the Lady's voice at all, hers being low and rounded and full, and his just being full.

Wishart actually held out the longest, until the breezes lifted the child onto his back. The baby crowed his delight, and if you could at that moment have seen the look in Wishart's old pearly eyes, you would have been sure they had turned to oceans themselves. He trotted around the inner path, past the herb garden, stepping over rockery plants with a lightness he hadn't shown in years.

The Lady changed the baby's clothes and fed him pap she mixed herself, and wiped both his face and his bottom as if that were something she had always wanted to do. And she sang to him as she cleaned, songs like "Dance to Your Daddy, My Little Laddie" and "Trot, Trot to Boston," which hadn't even been invented yet. And "Western Wind," which had.

Eventually, after months of squabbling, they settled on Waverly as his name.

"Because the waves brought him," Infanta said, looking down fondly into his crib.

As long as Waverly was a baby and then a young child, there was no trouble in the Lady's garden. After all, except for uprooting some of the slighter plants—to see what held them to the ground—Waverly was a good boy, if overly curious. Of course curiosity was not something either the Lady or the unicorns really understood. But they realized, if somewhat begrudgingly, that curiosity would serve young Waverly in his education, and so they did not stifle it.

By the time he was ten and had gone through "What's that?" and "Why's that?" and on to "Why not?," however, they had all begun to lose patience with him. With their sense of time, it seemed only yesterday that they had drawn baby Waverly up from the basket, though to Waverly it was ages and ages earlier.

Where, they wondered, *is the sweet-smelling, charming, compliant infant we fell in love with? And who is this loud, boisterous, dirty boy who has taken his place?* And slowly, though they didn't mean to, they all fell out of love with him. Just a little.

Just enough.

Now, Waverly did not know what was happening, but he certainly felt that something was. One moment everyone—Lady and unicorns and breezes—were all lovely to him, giving him whatever he asked for and praising him. And then suddenly they said "No!" all the time. "No, you cannot make a fortress in the rockery garden." "No, you cannot put a house up in the apple tree." "No, you cannot scale the wall." "No, you cannot . . . must not . . . shall not . . . may not . . ." to everything that seemed even the slightest bit interesting or exciting or dangerous.

So Waverly did what every child of ten does. He did it all anyway.

Neither the Lady nor the unicorns knew the slightest thing about giving out punishments. It was not in their makeup. So they did what they had done before Waverly had ever arrived. Wishart started listening only to the sound of the Ocean. Tartary listened only to the Lady's voice. Infanta listened only to the sounds of the Earth growing. And the Lady—she worked in the garden, she kept the great house clean, and she spoke to Waverly only when forced to. When forced to say, once again, "No!"

So it should not have been surprising—though it was—that on the morning of Waverly's sixteenth birthday (or at least the morning of the anniversary of the sixteenth year since he had been drawn up out of the sea) they were all awakened by the sound of loud chopping. When they got out to the garden, there was Waverly, an axe in hand. He had just finished cutting down the apple tree and was busy hollowing out the trunk for a boat.

"A boat?" the Lady asked, for she knew right away what he was doing, her prescience working as well as her eyes. "And where did you learn about boats?"

"Where I learned about the Ocean and where I learned about the World," Waverly answered sensibly. "In your library."

"But the apple tree was the oldest thing of all," the Lady said.

"And I am the newest," Waverly said. "Would you have had me make a boat from stone?"

"We wouldn't have had you make a boat at all," the Lady said. "Would we?" she asked the unicorns.

Wishart did not answer, for he was listening only to the Ocean, which was issuing a strange siren call. Tartary did not answer, for she was waiting for the Lady's own answer. And Infanta was too busy weeping over the demise of the apple tree.

Still, they didn't stop the boy, because he was already halfway through building the boat. And besides, they didn't know how.

It took him three days to make the boat and rig a sail, just as he had seen in one of the books in the Lady's library. And that very night, without so much as a good-bye, he was gone with the boat over the wall. They had no idea how he had managed; they had had no idea he was so resourceful.

The Lady mourned his leaving in her own way, digging up plants and moving them about—the Autumn crocus three times, until they died from all the changes.

Tartary and Infanta wandered the garden disconsolately, their heads so low they plowed furrows in the soil with their horns. But for the longest time, it looked as if Wishart hadn't even noticed the boy was gone. He just listened, ever more intently, at the northeastern gate to the sounds of the Ocean.

And then one morning, a gale blowing out upon the Ocean, Wishart roused in a sudden and inexplicable fury and beat upon the gate with his feet and plunged his horn again and again into the wood. At last the gate broke open from the savage attack, swung wide, and in rushed the angry sea.

The waters covered the garden and the house. The Lady and the unicorns were swept away in a great swirl of foam as pearly white as horn. And after the waters settled again, all that could be seen was the topmost part of the southwestern gate, the one closest to the World. And there, at low tide ever after, a black-backed gull sat, turning its head curiously at each passing breeze.

Of course that is not entirely the end of the story. I could not bear if that were so. Wishart and Tartary and Infanta became the very first narwhales, of course, those wonderful sleek whales with the long, twisting single horns.

The Lady built a new garden, this one under the Ocean, with bright anemones clinging to coral beds, like rockeries.

And Waverly, in the shape of a porpoise, comes to visit them every day and twice on Tuesdays, as regular as clockwork. Or so I like to think. And if you think there is a different ending, you will have to tell it yourself.

41

I was talking to my editor on the phone about this book, and mentioned that I wanted to do a story or poem about a narwhale hunt. In passing I said, "Or maybe a song." And then it struck me, a song was what I really wanted to do, like one of the old forecastle ballads the whalers sang.

I got my facts about the hunting of narwhales in part from Eve Bunting's Sea World Book of Whales, *which told me, among other things, that narwhales are found only in the waters of the north near the edges of the ice, and that a narwhale is usually twelve to sixteen feet from head to tail. The tusk, though, is another eight feet long.*

The Hunting of the Narwhale

In the year of our Lord eighteen fifty and four,
We set sail on the ship *Northern Queen.*
Our Captain was known for the breadth of his lore
And the Master was said to be mean.

The Cookie was quick with his knife, we'd been told,
Though he cooked up a wonderful stew,
And we would be richer than Midas of old,
Captain promised, before we were through.

    So it's off to the north where the chilly winds blow,
    And the unicorn fish is a-swimming below,
    Near the blue-and-white edge of the massive ice floe,
    We are hunting the one-horned whale.

Seems that way in the east there's a brisk-running trade
For that ivory tusk, for that horn.

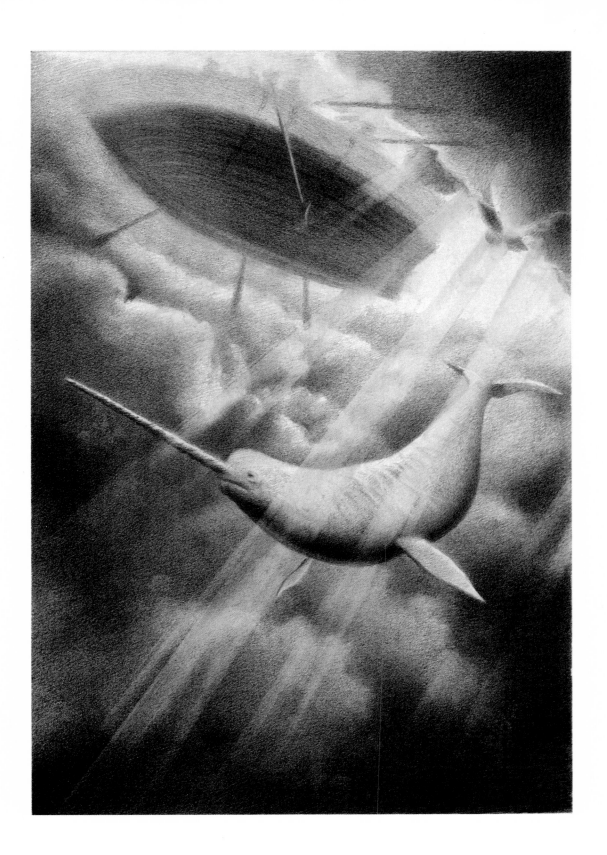

There it's pounded and powdered and then it is made
Into potion of "true unicorn."

Now you know and I know the horn is a tooth
And it comes from the jaw of a whale.
But far in the east there's a far different truth
Where the tusk has a mighty good sale.

    So it's off to the north where the chilly winds blow,
    And the unicorn fish is a-swimming below,
    Near the blue-and-white edge of the massive ice floe,
    We are hunting the one-horned whale.

We'd sailed to the veriest ends of the earth
When we sighted the first of the ice.
The ship took a turn and I fell off my berth
And then managed to slip once or twice.

But I got up above and I heard the great yell
Of the boy who was up in the crow.
We spotted the backs of a pod straight from hell
That was crowding a crooked ice floe.

    So it's off to the north where the chilly winds blow,
    And the unicorn fish is a-swimming below,
    Near the blue-and-white edge of the massive ice floe,
    We are hunting the one-horned whale.

We set out three boats and I rowed in the third,
Our harpooners all ready to fire.

Far overhead shrieked full dozens of birds
As the best of us started to tire.

The pod of the unicorn fish swam before
With their tusks piercing straight through the brine.
We leaned our strong backs once again to the oars
And I counted the whale that was mine.

    So it's off to the north where the chilly winds blow,
    Where the unicorn fish is a-swimming below,
    Near the blue-and-white edge of the massive ice floe,
    We are hunting the one-horned whale.

But the horn of the narwhale is not meant for fun,
It is sharper than any knight's sword.
We were all of us swimming before they were done
And not all of us got back on board.

The helmsman was missing and so was the lad
Who had called out "Whale ho!" from the crow.
And missing as well were the boats we had had,
And the Cookie was missing also.

    So it's off to the north where the chilly winds blow,
    Where the unicorn fish is a-swimming below,
    Near the blue-and-white edge of the massive ice floe,
    We are hunting the one-horned whale.

The *Queen*, she limped homeward with half of her crew
With the Master most times at the wheel.

Jack Johnson and I traded turns making stew
And nobody had a good meal.

We never got paid and I still have bad dreams
But at least I am safe on the shore.
The unicorn fish ain't as sweet as it seems
So I'm not going hunting no more.

But it's off to the north where the chilly winds blow,
Where the unicorn fish still is swimming below,
Near the blue-and-white edge of that massive ice floe,
You can go hunt that damned one-horned whale.

Bruce Coville, one of my dearest friends, was working on a unicorn anthology and asked me to write a story for it. Now, I love to accommodate my friends, really I do. But I had no ideas at all when I sat down at the typewriter to do as he asked.

"The Boy Who Drew Unicorns" was a title that suddenly popped into my head. Why? I don't know, though I am mammothly jealous of anyone who can draw; I collect art and revere artists. And the story that followed flowed out quickly. Normally my stories take days, weeks, sometimes even years to be finished. Not this one.

In unicorn lore the horn heals all wounds. Unfortunately, the people who believed that also believed a ground-up unicorn horn could be used medicinally as a powder, poultice, or potion. Lacking any real unicorns, there grew up a brisk trade in narwhale horns, which contributed to a deep drop in the narwhale population. You might also want to know that the name Phillip really does mean "a lover of horses" and that Ms. Wynne is named after my friend Diana Wynne Jones, one of my favorite fantasy writers. Without realizing it, I used the notion of the original "thrush" from the garden of Eden in this story as I did in "Unicorn Tapestry," lines from a poem I had written in college and later turned into a song. Authors are great recyclers. Finally, the park carousel and its glade are modeled after the one in New York City's Central Park and based on my childhood memories. I am sure that this carousel looks nothing like the real one. Memory is like that.

The Boy Who Drew Unicorns

There was once a boy who drew unicorns. Even before he knew their names, he caught them mane and hoof and horn on his paper. And they were white beasts and grey, black beasts and brown, galloping across the brown supermarket bags. He didn't know what to call them at first, but he knew what they called him: Phillip, a lover of horses, Philly, Phil.

Now, children, there is going to be a new boy in class today. His name is Philadelphia Carew.

Philadelphia? That's a city name, not a kid's name.

Hey, my name is New York.

Call me Chicago.

I got a cousin named India, does that count?

Enough, children. This young man is very special. You must try to be kind to him. He'll be very shy. And he's had a lot of family problems.

I got family problems too, Ms. Wynne. I got a brother and he's a big problem.

Joseph, that's enough.

He's six feet tall. That's a very big problem.

Now you may all think you have problems, but this young man has more than most. You see, he doesn't talk.

Not ever?

No. Not now. Not for several years. That's close enough to ever, I think.

Bet you'd like it if we didn't talk. Not for several years.

No, I wouldn't like that at all, though if I could shut you up for several hours, Joseph. . . .

Ooooh, Joey, she's got you!

"What is the good of such drawing, Philadelphia?" his mother said. "If you have to draw, draw something useful. Draw me some money or some groceries or a new man, one who doesn't beat us. Draw us some better clothes or a bed for yourself. Draw me a job."

But he drew only unicorns: horselike, goatlike, deerlike, lamblike, bull-like, things he had seen in books. Four-footed, silken swift, with the single golden horn. His corner of the apartment was papered with them.

When's he coming, Ms. Wynne?

Today. After lunch.

Does he look weird, too?

He's not weird, Joseph. He's special. And I expect you—all of you—to act special.

She means we shouldn't talk.

No, Joseph, I mean you need to think before you talk. Think what it must be like not to be able to express yourself.

I'd use my hands.

Does he use his hands, Ms. Wynne?

I don't know.

Stupid, only deaf people do that. Is he deaf?

No.

Is there something wrong with his tongue?

No.

Why doesn't he talk, then?

Why do you think?

Maybe he likes being special.

That's a very interesting idea, Joseph.

Maybe he's afraid.

Afraid to talk? Don't be dumb.

Now, Joseph, that's another interesting idea, too. What are you afraid of, children?

Snakes, Ms. Wynne.

I hate spiders.

I'm not afraid of anything!

Nothing at all, Joseph?

Maybe my big brother. When he's mad.

49

In school he drew unicorns down the notebook page, next to all his answers. He drew them on his test papers. On the bathroom walls. They needed no signature. Everyone knew he had made them. They were his thumbprints. They were his heartbeats. They were his scars.

Oooooh, he's drawing them things again.
Don't you mess up my paper, Mr. Philadelphia Carew.
Leave him alone. He's just a dummy.
Horses don't have horns, dummy.
Here comes Ms. Wynne.
If you children will get back in your seats and stop crowding around Philly. You've all seen him draw unicorns before. Now listen to me, and I mean you, too, Joseph. Fold your hands and lift those shining faces to me. Good. We are going on a field trip this afternoon. Joseph, sit in your seat properly and leave Philly's paper alone. A field trip to Chevril Park. Not now, Joseph, get back in your seat. We will be going after lunch. And *after your spelling test.*
Ooooh, what test, Ms. Wynne?
You didn't say there was going to be a test.

The park was a place of green glades. It had trees shaped like Fudgesicles with the chocolate running down the sides. It had trees like umbrellas that moved mysteriously in the wind. There were hidden ponds and secret streams and moist pathways between, lined with rings of white toadstools and trillium the color of blood. Cooing pigeons walked boldly on the pavement. But in the quiet underbrush hopped little brown birds with white throats. Silent throats.

From far away came a strange, magical song. It sounded like a melody mixed with a gargle, a tune touched by a laugh. It creaked, it hesitated, then it sang again. He had never heard anything like it before.

I hear it, Ms. Wynne. I hear the merry-go-round.

And what does it sound like, children?

It sounds lumpy.

Don't be dumb. It sounds upsy-downsy.

It sounds happy and sad.

Joseph, what do you think it sounds like?

Like another country. Like "The Twilight Zone."

Very good, Joseph. And see, Philly is agreeing with you. And strangely, Joseph, you are right. Merry-go-rounds or carousels are from another country, another world. The first ones were built in France in the late 1700s. The best hand-carved animals still are made in Europe. What kind of animals do you think you'll see on this merry-go-round?

Horses.

Lions.

Tigers.

Camels.

Don't be dumb—camels.

There are too! I been here before. And elephants.

He saw unicorns galloping around and around, a whole herd of them. And now he saw his mistake. They were not like horses or goats or deer or lambs or bulls. They were like—themselves. And with the sun slanting on them from beyond the trees, they were like rainbows, all colors and no colors at all.

Their mouths were open and they were calling. That was the magical song he had heard before. A strange, shimmery kind of cry, not like horses or goats or deer or lambs or bulls; more musical, with a strange rise and fall to each phrase.

He tried to count them as they ran past. Seven, fifteen, twenty-one . . . he couldn't contain them all. Sometimes they doubled back and he was forced to count them again. And again. He settled for the fact that it was a herd of unicorns. No. *Herd* was too ordinary a word for what they were. Horses came in herds. And cows. But unicorns—there had to be a special word for them all together. Suddenly he knew what it was, as if they had told him so in their wavery song. He was watching a *surprise* of unicorns.

Look at old weird Philly. He's just staring at the merry-go-round. Come on, Mr. Philadelphia Chicago New York L.A. Carew. Go on up and ride. They won't bite.

Joseph, keep your mouth shut and you might be able to hear something.

What, Ms. Wynne?

You might hear the heart's music, Joseph. That's a lot more interesting than the flapping of one's own mouth.

What does that mean, Ms. Wynne?

It means shut up, Joseph.

Ooooh, she got you, Joey.

It means shut up, Denise, too, I bet.

All of you, mouths shut, ears open. We're going for a ride.

We don't have any money, Ms. Wynne.

That's all taken care of. Everyone pick out a horse or a whatever. Mr. Frangipanni, the owner of this carousel, can't wait all day.

Dibs on the red horse.

I got the gray elephant.

Mine's the white horse.

No, Joseph, can't you see Philly has already chosen that one?

But heroes always ride the white horse. And he isn't any kind of hero.

Choose another one, Joseph.

Aaaah, Ms. Wynne, that's not fair.

Why not take the white elephant, Joseph. Hannibal, a great hero of history,
marched across the high Alps on elephants to capture Rome.
Wow—did he really?
Really, Joseph.
Okay. Where's Rome?
Who knows where Rome is? I bet Mr. Frangipanni does.
Then ask Mr. Frangipanni!
Italy, Ms. Wynne.
Italy is right. Time to mount up. That's it. We're all ready, Mr. Frangipanni.

The white flank scarcely trembled, but he saw it. *Do not be afraid,*
he thought. *I couldn't ever hurt you.* He placed his hand gently on the
tremor and it stopped.

Moving up along the length of the velvety beast, he saw the
arched neck ahead of him, its blue veins like tiny rivers branching
under the angel-hair mane.

One swift leap and he was on its back. The unicorn turned its head
to stare at him with its amber eyes. The horn almost touched his knee.
He flinched, pulling his knee up close to his chest. The unicorn turned
its head back and looked into the distance.

He could feel it move beneath him, the muscles bunching and
flattening as it walked. Then with that strange wild cry, the unicorn
leaped forward and began to gallop around and around the glade.

He could sense others near him, catching movement out of the
corners of his eyes. Leaning down, he clung to the unicorn's mane.
They ran through day and into the middle of night, till the stars fell
like snow behind them. He heard a great singing in his head and heart
and he suddenly felt as if the strength of old kings were running in his
blood. He threw his head back and laughed aloud.

————

Boy, am I dizzy.
My elephant was the best.
I had a red pony. Wow, did we fly!
Everyone dismounted? Now, tell me how you felt.

He slid off the silken side, feeling the solid earth beneath his feet. There was a buzz of voices around him, but he ignored them all. Instead, he turned back to the unicorn and walked toward its head. Standing still, he reached up and brought its horn down until the point rested on his chest. The golden whorls were hard and cold beneath his fingers. And if his fingers seemed to tremble ever so slightly, it was no more than how the unicorn's flesh had shuddered once under the fragile shield of its skin.

He stared into the unicorn's eyes, eyes of antique gold so old, he wondered if they had first looked on the garden where the original thrush had sung the first notes from a hand-painted bush.

Taking his right hand off the horn, he sketched a unicorn in the air between them.

As if that were all the permission it needed, the unicorn nodded its head. The horn ripped his light shirt, right over the heart. He put his left palm over the rip. The right he held out to the unicorn. It nuzzled his hand and its breath was moist and warm.

Look, look at Philly's shirt.
Ooooh, there's blood.
Let me through, children. Thank you, Joseph, for helping him get down. Are you hurt, Philly? Now don't be afraid. Let me see. I could never hurt you. Why, I think there's a cut there. Mr. Frangipanni, come quick. Have you any bandages? The boy is hurt. It's a tiny wound but there's lots of blood, so it may be very deep. Does it hurt, dear?

55

No.

Brave boy. Now be still till Mr. Frangipanni comes.
He spoke, Ms. Wynne. Philly spoke.
Joseph, do be still, I have enough trouble without you . . .
But he spoke, Ms. Wynne. He said "No."
Don't be silly, Joseph.
But he did. He spoke. Didn't you, Philly?
Yes.

Yes.

He turned and looked.

The unicorn nodded its head once and spoke in that high, wavering magical voice. "THE HORN HEALS."

He repeated it.

Yes. The horn heals.
He spoke! He spoke!
I'll just clean this wound, Philly, don't move. Why—that's strange. There's
some blood, but only an old scar. Are you sure you're all right, dear?
Yes.

Yes.

As he watched, the unicorn dipped its horn to him once, then whirled away, disappearing into the dappled light of the trees. He wondered if he would ever capture it right on paper. It was nothing like the sketches he had drawn before. Nothing. But he would try.

Yes, Ms. Wynne, an old scar healed. I'm sure.

The Drabble Project was the brainchild of a pair of British writers, Rob Meade and David Wake. They asked one hundred authors to each write a fantasy or science fiction story of exactly one hundred words. (The title didn't count.) I was one of the authors when they did a second book with the same ground rules.

Then an American science fiction fan publisher, Ed Meskys, decided to go them one better and asked a number of us to do a fifty-word—no more, no less—story. Again the title didn't count. Here is a fifty-word tale.

Stories about unicorn hunts first appeared in the fourth century A.D. The bait was always a pure young maiden sitting under a tree. The unicorn would put its head in her lap and, thus ensnared, was an easy target for the hunters.

The Promise

Deep in the forest she waited. Not even a stray wind broke the silence.

When she heard footsteps, she looked up, sighing deeply, not caring the hunters heard, her long wait over.

When the blanched, weary girl sat, the unicorn gratefully moved forward, putting her head into the promised lap.

One of the saddest scenes in literature was written by T. H. White. It is a unicorn hunt in his Once and Future King. *And I have always wondered how anyone, gazing at that beauty, could kill it. Youngsters going on their first deer hunt have been known to get "buck fever," which causes them to tremble so much they cannot shoot.*

The idea of pure maidens being used to trap unicorns goes all the way back to a text called Physiologus *(which means "The Naturalist"), a collection of stories and fables and descriptions of real and imagined animals so old that it was repudiated in* A.D. *496 as a work of heresy. In many ways, the old stories are allegories of Christianity, with the girl in the role of Mary, the mother of God. But there are other stories in which the girl plays a more sinister role, tempting the pure unicorn to follow her. Whichever theme is used, a maiden involved in the "Holy Hunt" is one of the most popular parts of all unicorn lore.*

I started this story as a 100-worder. At its first draft it was 172 words, and it kept begging to be longer, not shorter. What I think it has become is a prose poem, a form somewhere in between a lyric poem and a piece of prose.

The last line has not changed from that first draft.

The Hunt

We had to muzzle the dogs, for they longed to sing out when on the chase. The spears we had sharpened with stones. Bartholomew had a bow and Martin his father's sword. We had a catch-basin—Lady Elizabeth's good cobalt bowl—for the blood.

Martin's sister, little Miriam, came along as the bait. She did not come for love. There were copper coins in each of her hands. She held them so tightly, the king's face had left its impression on each of her palms.

We made her sit under the oak, feet tucked beneath her skirts. The broad trunk made a good purchase for her back. She was too young to sit still for long. We warned her to be quiet; we hoped she would sleep.

Then we hid ourselves, each with a hound, in the nearby copse, remembering the stories, remembering the songs. It was our first hunt.

When the unicorn came at last, picking through the wildflowers on dainty, cloven feet, it was so silken white and shining, I dropped my spear in awe. Martin put his head into his hands and wept at its beauty. Bartholomew's bow, unstrung, fell to the ground. Even the dogs, in the face of such mystery, refused to growl.

Little Miriam laughed with delight when the beast put its head in her lap. She leaned over and kissed it on the forehead, at the base of the horn.

We let her keep the coins.

I am not sure when I wrote this. I found it in my files. The phrase "silken swift" I love and stole, quite deliberately, from the best unicorn story I know, Theodore Sturgeon's "The Silken-Swift," which I read as a teenager in his collection E Pluribus Unicorn *and never forgot. Can you find how many times I've used it in this collection?*

The Unicorn Leaves

Deep, deep, deep in the cool
Forest, by a mirror pool,
Lives the silken swift,
Lives the marble gift
With a spiral horn.

Someday you may see him pass
As a shadow; hear the grass
Bend his steps. And hush!
Watch the poolside rushes
Parted by the horn.

The water bursts as if a gale
Started from his golden nail,
Bids them part. Then the sounds
Of horse and hounds,
And in a moment, he is gone.

Bartholomaeus Anglicus was a thirteenth-century English monk who wrote about animals—mixing mythic with real—in a mammoth compendium entitled De Proprietatibus Rerum. *He did, in fact, say, "An unicorn is a right cruel beast." Then he maundered on and on about rhinoceros and monoceros and others in quite a boring fashion. I doubt he actually traveled the countryside lecturing dukes and their hunts, though. He probably stayed quietly in his monastery, scribbling away.*

Ctesias, on the other hand, did travel. A Greek historian from the fourth century B.C., *he penned the first written account of a unicorn after having visited the Persian court. What he saw there might have been an oryx, a kind of gazelle with arching horns. Or even the gigantic aurochs, or wild buffalo, twelve feet long and seven feet high, extinct by the sixteenth century. He certainly didn't see a unicorn.*

Some of the hunting stuff for this story I got from Gustave Flaubert's odd little fairy tale "The Legend of Saint Julian Hospitaler" and Beryl Rowland's equally odd "Animals with Human Faces." The rest of the story is pure fiction. That is, I admit it is fiction. Bartholomaeus and Ctesias insisted that what they wrote was fact.

De Natura Unicorni

"The unicorn," Brother Bartholomaeus said, "is a right cruel beast. He files his horn against stone. There is the rhinoceros unicorn, big and fat and slow, but deadly nonetheless. And the monoceros, more like a horse in its body. Though in the Indias, there is one more like to an ass, only less bold and fierce. There are seven clear references to the unicorn in Scripture." As he spoke, he pointed to a chart that he had leaned against the wall. A small wind through the narrow window caught the edge of the vellum, riffling it a bit. Young James, the duke's son, stood up and set his hand against the chart, holding it steady. He was that kind of boy.

Richard studied the chart. It was probably not entirely accurate. Brother Bartholomaeus was good in theory but his drawing left much to be desired. Still, he had spent years in the East, where unicorns were plentiful. And as Duke William wanted his people to make this year's Great Hunt for the beast, one having been sighted weeks earlier by a woodcutter, they were all diligently studying the nature of the unicorn. Even Gregory, who found diligence in anything but wagering a bore.

"What about its eyesight?" the duke asked. The men of the Hunt nodded at the question.

"Keen," Brother Bartholomaeus said, his shortest statement so far.

"And hearing?"

"Equal." Brother Bartholomaeus smiled at young James in thanks and rolled up his scroll slowly. The wind now puzzled the good friar's tonsure. "But as for its sense of smell . . ."

"Like a horse's, I'll wager," Gregory whispered to Richard. "Or like an ass's."

". . . it is more a horse's than a deer's," Brother Bartholomaeus continued placidly.

Gregory grinned. "You owe me a copper piece."

"I did not agree to any such," Richard said. "I know better."

Gregory shook his head, but his grin did not fade. "Then I will wager I get a unicorn horn before you do, and sit higher at the table of honor."

"Now, that," Richard said, knowing himself the better archer, "is a wager I *will* take." He licked his thumb and held it up. Gregory did likewise. Then to seal their bet, they touched thumbs. No one seemed to notice, except for the duke, who noticed everything. But he said nothing, so that was all right.

At dinner, Brother Bartholomaeus continued lecturing through every course. He did not stop talking even when flinging the meat bones over his shoulder for the Breton hounds.

"The great Ctesias," he said, "speaks of the powers of the horn. Powdered, it is a known cure-all. And of course, a surety against poison."

The duke nodded. For as powerful a man as he, with many enemies about, such a medicine was worth an entire city.

The boys, however, had stopped listening by the salad service and had taken to playing mumblety-peg with their knives on the wooden benches. Only bits and pieces from the monk's conversation drifted down the table to them.

When the servants had cleared away the crockery and there was nothing left to do but go to bed or listen to even more of Brother Bartholomaeus, they elected for bed, up in the tower. James, being the duke's only son and therefore his heir, had his own apartment one floor below Richard and Gregory's. But frequently he escaped the ministrations of his manservant and his tutor and went up the secret stair to spend the night with his friends. Young lordlings, they were seven years older than he and therefore held a great fascination for him.

"Do you really think there's a unicorn in the New?" James asked, sitting cross-legged on Richard's bed. He meant the New Forest, so named—of course—because it was the oldest forest in the dukedom.

"Your father certainly seems to think so," Richard said carefully.

"I mean a *real* unicorn, one that is silken and white, with an ivory horn right dab in the middle of its head." James said. "And not just some deer a peasant saw sideways in the moonlight. No one's seen one in ages and Mereton thinks they are all dead." James was very keen on the Hunt, this being the first year he was to be let on one, free of his leading strings.

"Mereton is a tutor, not a hunter," Gregory said. "I bet you a copper he wouldn't know the front end of a hinny from the back end of a hind, much less the fabled unicorn."

James threw a pillow at Gregory, who laughed.

"Stranger things have been found in the New," Richard said in his cautious way. He didn't have to add what strange things. Their heads—monstrous shapes—lined the stairs of the hunting hall.

"He's awfully certain . . ." James said. "Brother Bartholomaeus."

"He's awfully pompous," Richard rejoined.

"He's awfully fat!" said Gregory, which was what they had all been thinking and with that they fell over on the beds, laughing so loudly that the manservant, Bertram, came in and cautioned them. "My lords, if the duke . . ."

It should have been enough. Indeed, no one said anything more about the friar, but Gregory got off his bed and stuffed a pillow beneath his tunic and staggered about as though he were too fat to walk properly. He opened and shut his mouth as if talking without cessation, and that set them to laughing again.

Bertram came back to the door, and behind him was the tutor, Mereton. With an almost imperceptible nod, Mereton separated James from the older boys. James may have been the duke's son but, at seven, he was still biddable. He went downstairs to bed.

They studied about the unicorn for two days more, with Brother Bartholomaeus and his charts and a rather large tome by "the great Ctesias," as the fat friar called him.

"Great bloody book at any rate," whispered Gregory, though Richard blanched at his swearing.

At last, even Duke William got tired of it, sending the friar home to the abbey on a slow, fat jennet whose saddlebags were packed with gifts of cheese and wine and embroidered altar cloths. "Let him bother the abbot with his lectures," the duke was overheard saying to his new young wife, Lady Ann. "I think we know enough now for the Hunt."

Then all the castle turned to the real preparations: Arrows were newly fletched, swords freshly honed, spearheads tightened on their shafts. Journeybread was baked in the castle ovens, wine poured into skins. Saddles were oiled, bridles polished. It was a manly time, and young James fairly quivered with excitement till the night before they were to leave on the Hunt, when he had to be put to bed and made to drink a blackberry tisane to quiet him. *Perhaps*, Richard thought, *he isn't as steady as all that.*

Hunt morning, the sky outside was the color of barley.

> *Pearly skies*
> *Herald a surprise,*

warned Old Langton at the gate as they rode out. But as he always forecast disasters, they ignored him.

Though it was early Autumn, it was cold enough for the breath to stream out of the horses' nostrils in gouts.

"Almost as if they were dragons," James cried.

His father smiled at him indulgently. Dragons had been extinct in the land for over one hundred years. Turning to the master of his Hunt, the duke commented, "Not much wind. So it won't catch us that way." He nodded at the master. "Lead on, then."

The master, Miles Cavendish by name, headed them west, then north, to the edge of the New Forest: the men on their great-footed horses, Richard and Gregory on small geldings, and young James on his pony. The master of hounds, a dour Caledonian named McBrane, and his pack of greys, Bretons, and two mastiffs the color of flame trotted alongside.

They traveled over a final great meadow, the grass still so fresh and tender that all of them—even Duke William—had some trouble with the horses wanting to stop and graze. Then they passed a patch of nettle and elderberry and a stand of ash crowning a gully. Overhead, crows wheeled about in the sky, warning of their coming. Under the horses' heavy feet, sorrel and buttercup and even long, bendy plantains were crushed. At last the Hunt came into the forest proper, where great branches of holm oak closed over their heads, making a canopy of leaves that held out the sun.

It was cold in the New Forest; it smelled of damp and mold. To the right, a pretty little stream stumbled over stones and rocks and even an occasional boulder, but quietly.

The cold and damp and quiet seemed to get into everything. From the moment they entered under the interlacing of oak leaves, not a word was spoken. Even the horses stopped snorting.

"Magic," young James whispered under his breath, clutching his reins tightly.

Magic, Richard thought, and said a quick Te Deum to himself.

"Magic." Gregory heard it just as if someone had spoken it aloud, but of course no one had. He wagered to himself his next three coppers, though what he wanted to wager about wasn't exactly clear; still, it lent him some comfort.

Cavendish raised a hand and they all stopped, duke and son, lord-lings, archers, hunters, hounds. He looked about as if judging the timbre of the forest and the weight of it. As if he kenned something more from the leaves and bark and boles of trees than the rest of them did. Then, having made up his mind about something, Cavendish signaled them toward the right-hand path, and down it they went in a tumbling mob, startling wood pigeons who clattered noisily up from the forest floor into the oaks for safety.

They rode on and on, through lunch and well into the afternoon, till Richard wondered whether they were still going *into* the forest or already starting *out* again. They walked, then trotted, then walked again. Richard didn't say a word, of course. To do so would have been to disgrace himself and his father, who had sent him off to Duke William's service, lord to lord.

At last they came to another fork in the forest road, and this time Cavendish got down off his horse. He kicked about in the undergrowth for a while. Twice he bent over and picked up some fewmets, bringing them to his nose to test their freshness. Then he crumpled them in his hand before letting the pieces fall to the ground.

"Old, my lord," he said to the duke. "And roe deer at that."

"Not unicorn, then?" the duke asked.

"Not here. And not back where the peasant reported it either."

"Should we ride on, then?" the duke asked.

Cavendish looked around, then up at the trees and, higher, to a small patch of sky. "Make camp," he said, "my lord."

Richard noticed that everyone relaxed at that. Secretly, he was relieved he was not the only one.

After a spare dinner—journeybread, a brace of rabbits, and a half dozen pigeons brought in by Cavendish and his three helpers—they sat about the fire and the men traded stories of past Hunts. The stories all ended happily, though Richard knew that was not always the case.

Still, on the first night, it would have been considered ill luck to tell anything else. So the boys heard of grand Hunts in which bear and boar and stag and grouse were brought back by the hundredweight, tied onto sledges made of silver birch branches and pulled by the horses.

Later, when the fire had burned down to embers and young James was asleep in his father's tent, Cavendish sang a strange song. He had a surprisingly sweet tenor voice and the song was unlike any Richard had ever heard, full of descending notes. It made him both angry and sad at the same time. The chorus was the same throughout, and after the sixth or seventh verse, they all joined in, but quietly, so as not to wake the sleeping James.

> The horn, the horn, the spiral horn
> As thick as a tree, as sharp as a thorn,
> As long as a life, as bloody as morn,
> It will pierce the heart of the hunter.

Richard fell asleep dreaming the words, but he could not—in his dream—identify the hunter.

In the morning, they carefully buried all signs of their encampment, mounted, and rode on. This time, though, Cavendish walked before them, patiently sorting through signs: fox tracks, wolf scratchings, and the now-multitudinous droppings of stag and hare. They made little headway, however, for the forest was thick and the pathway grown over with brambles.

By the end of the second day, even the Duke was showing his impatience. Only young James seemed oblivious to the growing dark mood of the Hunt. Richard thought it might be because this was his

71

first such outing and James was afraid to say anything to compromise a second.

But Gregory had no such fear. "This is foolery," he said, his voice dripping scorn. "We shoot at nothing, so as not to frighten the unicorn. But how can we? The unicorn is a right cruel beast indeed. Cruel enough to keep out of sight." And when Richard tried to hush him up, Gregory continued even louder. "My back hurts from sitting this bloody horse. And that's not the only part of me that hurts." It was a wonder the duke did not call him down. Richard suspected it was because the duke felt the same way.

As a result, the second night's encampment was less jolly than the first's. There was no singing that evening, and precious few stories, except for tales about life within the castle walls, a life that now seemed sweeter and easier than when they had left.

Richard had the same dream that night: the cruel unicorn horn piercing the heart of the hunter. As in the first dream, though he could see the face of the beast quite well, he could not make out the features of the wounded man.

The third day dawned exceeding grey, the sun the color of old pearl. Richard suddenly recalled Langton's prophecy. The dreams of the last two nights wrapped around him like a shroud; he could not shrug off the feeling of impending disaster. But to say so aloud would mark him in the Hunt's eyes as a feeble creature, fit only for the fireside. He remained silent.

The Hunt rode on. Around them the wood grew strangely still. Richard found himself shivering uncontrollably, as if he had caught a chill. At that very moment, Cavendish held up his right hand.

"Sign," he mouthed.

They dismounted and gathered around him.

"See," he said, pointing to the ground where hoofprints scumbled together in the fresh earth. "Most likely a male. They live in strife with their own kind, except during rut. The females go in herds, but not the males."

Richard could not remember Brother Bartholomaeus remarking on this, and Cavendish, as if he had read Richard's mind, said, "I had it from my dad, who was master afore me. He hunted a licorne once." He used the old country name for the beast. "Didn't get it, though."

"We will have more luck," James cried out.

"From your young mouth to God's old ear," whispered the master of hounds, signing the cross three times over his broad chest.

They made a great half circle then, for a sweep through the tangled woods, to drive ahead of them any beast so the dogs—now eager and straining at their leads—could bring it down. The archers had arrows nocked and ready. Only Duke William, James, Richard, and Gregory, being of the nobility, rode the final quartering. And Cavendish, of course, that he might better direct the Hunt. And the master of hounds.

They started several hares, and the greyhounds tried to give chase, but the Bretons and mastiffs were of sterner stuff. Even when a covey of grouse flew up before them, clappering into the lightening air, they did not startle. But one young greyhound disgraced himself thoroughly by running behind the master and almost bringing him down with the leather lead.

And then, with a full belling cry, one of the Bretons leaped against his tether and the rest of the pack joined in, leader and chorus.

"Something big, my lord," the master of hounds cried.

"It's the licorne!" called Cavendish, who had a glimpse of white haunch. Richard saw it at the same moment and had a sudden taste of something both sharp and sour in his mouth, like death.

73

Quickly the dogs were unleashed and pack and men surged forward, a tide of terror, crying out after their prey.

"Halloooooooo!" Gregory shouted in a spirited voice.

The duke and Richard and the archers added their voices to his, but Cavendish and James remained silent. Then the Hunt crashed through the brush, heedless of nettles and briars tearing at their clothing and exposed skin. One man lost his boot and raced on regardless, in a kind of rolling gait. Richard's horse stumbled, righted itself, raced on.

The unicorn led them through a gnarl, then through a small copse of trees. Branches smacked at them as they rode; one even threatened to unseat James on his pony, but gamely he stayed on, though he sported a reddened cheek from the contact.

And then they broke through into a meadow that was covered with thousands of flowers, red and purple and yellow and blue, like a tapestry. There, unexpectedly, the unicorn turned to face them, its white face flecked with silvered foam. The afternoon sun shining down caught the gleam of its horn—not ivory, as Richard had expected, but a pure beaten gold.

The beast was so strange and beautiful, Richard drew in a deep and painful breath before reining in his horse. Then he reached for his bow and two arrows.

In that moment, the dogs were on the unicorn. The greyhounds, being fastest, reached it first, harrying it right, then left. Almost disdainfully, the unicorn kept them at bay, lowering its head and parrying them with its horn. It only nicked one of the older greyhounds, but it caught the young, inexperienced dog—the one who had tangled the master—with a full thrust in the belly. Without a sound, the dog rolled over on its back, frantically licking at the blood and spilled intestines, before it died.

At the sight of the blood, the Bretons sprang forward, going for the unicorn's nose. A circling mastiff managed to sink its teeth for a moment into the beast's haunch, but it could not hold. The blood it drew seemed twice as red as that which had spilled from the hound's belly.

James cried out, as if *he* were wounded and not the unicorn. In all the bustle of beast against beast, it was the only sound.

The duke dismounted and unsheathed his sword. These were his woods and his Hunt, and therefore—they all knew without being told—the honor of slaying the unicorn was his as well. But the others kept their bows and pikes ready, just in case.

As the duke drew toward the harried beast, it threw off all the dogs as though they were of no consequence at all. Two greys went down with opened bellies, and one of the Bretons was bleeding from the nose. The mastiff that had sunk its teeth into the unicorn's flank was now missing those teeth and half its jaw as well, from a back kick. Its partner, as if chastened by the sight, had slunk off to the back of the Hunt. No amount of urging by the master of hounds served to send it forward again.

Still the duke did not waver, and Richard and Gregory leaped from their own horses, ready to help, ready to loose their arrows through the blood-scented air.

As if only then noticing the men, the unicorn raised its head and stared at them. Richard was close enough to see that its eyes were the color of amber and seemed to have in them a light of understanding that was neither a beast's nor a man's but something else altogether, though in that hurly moment, he could not think what.

"You are mine," the duke said. His voice, so definite, so possessive, rang out unnaturally in the stilled meadow.

From somewhere far away, a cuckoopint suddenly began singing, and it seemed to Richard as sweet as if it had been singing in Heaven itself. He was transfixed by the song and, for a moment, could not move.

In that same moment, the unicorn lunged forward. With its horn, it knocked away the duke's sword as easily as if he were a boy playing his first game with the master of swords. The duke seemed dazed and stood there, his body now fully exposed to the spiral horn.

None of them moved, all equally ensorcelled by the song, except for young James. With a cry of "Father! I come!" he flung himself from his pony and stepped between the duke and the harrowing horn.

The horn plunged into the boy's breast, shredding the tunic. The sound of the material ripping started time again, like a swiftly flowing river.

Richard gasped, drew his bow, and let one and then a second arrow fly, without even waiting to take aim. They both went truly into the unicorn's broad chest. At the same time, Gregory's arrow sang into the white flank. The remaining mastiff ran from behind its master and flung itself onto the unicorn's neck, never minding the shuddering flesh beneath. And there it hung on grimly until the end.

That end was swift and sure and angry, for while the duke cradled his son in his arms, the rest of the Hunt thrust and hacked and slashed at the unicorn until it was black with its own blood and their fury. Even the Bretons and greys tore at its flesh, savaging it till there was nothing left of the white beauty.

Richard was sick from the savagery. He would have gone back into the woods and vomited till the smell and sight of the carnage were all purged from him, but he knew what the others would think if he did. So he swallowed it back down. Only when he was certain he was right again did he turn and look at the duke, who was still kneeling with his son in his arms.

Richard was not sure what he expected—what terror and what pain. But he was not prepared for the look of ecstasy on the faces of both father and son. When he ran closer, he saw that James was—unbelievably—not harmed in the slightest. Where the tunic lay open and torn, his bare chest manifested no sign of a wound. Rather, over his heart, the skin was incised with the sign of a cross, like an illumination in a Book of Hours.

"I do not understand," Richard whispered, turning to look back at the unicorn.

What lay there, ripped apart, was a great black beast, more like an ox or an Irish elk. Its skin—what he could still see of it—was ebony and ridged. Its legs were massive, like columns in a church. There was a single horn, fat and riddled with wormholes, protruding from its inelegant nose.

"Monoceros," said Cavendish, kicking at the carcass.

Richard glanced at the duke and James once more. They were gazing far beyond the dead beast to the other side of the meadow, and they were both smiling.

When he turned to follow their gaze, he thought he glimpsed something white and gleaming leaping into the trees. For a moment it was dappled with shadows. Then it was gone.

"Do you want the horn, my lord?" asked Cavendish.

The duke didn't answer at first. He set James down as gently as if the boy had been a young maid. Then he stood. "Of course," he said. "It may be proof against poison. Or at least, so my enemies will think. Besides, my good dogs and that great beast should not have died for aught."

They rode home the whole way, arriving well after midnight. In the morning, when it was announced that James would enter the monastery at Shrewsbury as an infant oblate, Richard was not surprised.

Gregory's eyes, though, widened at the announcement. "And I would have put a whole gold piece on his becoming as great a hunter as his father," he said. "Did you see how steady he held his ground?"

But Richard understood. The duke's new young wife could have many sons. Why would she want another woman's child as heir? And certainly anyone touched by God's own horn was marked forever. Richard knew this with certainty. For when he dreamed, as he did every night thereafter, he dreamed of the unicorn, white and golden and swift, running through the dappled trees of Paradise, with Richard running, frantically, after. And always he was too slow, too unsure, too unsteady to capture it for his own.

Unicorn lore has it that a pool where a unicorn drinks, or a pool in which a unicorn dips its horn, will be crystalline and pure. This poem, written when I was a senior at Smith College, came from an odd dream I had.

The Unicorn's Pool

Dreaming, I wake;
Deep, deep and cool,
Fed by no streams,
The unicorn's pool
Lies quiet, clear.

Here, in the woods, past hearing,
I have seen him,
Stately, silent, silken swift,
Surely the gift
Of a very good God.

God,
I had ridden so far,
So far for nothing,
I thought. But noting
A path, sun-dappled
And rippling,
A golden stream into the woods,
As in a dream
I followed.

How many paths
Have led me through woods
Warrened with houses?

But today,
Today I believed,
And believing,
Lived
To see him, silken, swift.

His head shifted
As I came near.
His horn pressed through my breast.
And now I rest,
Here, at the pool,
My blood the feeding stream,
And waking, I dream.

Surely he is the gift
Of a very good God.

My friend Christine Crow, a novelist and professor of French, lives across the street from me in Scotland. She lent me a copy of The Lore of the Unicorn *when I was there working on my book. My own copy was at home in Massachusetts. In* The Lore *is a fragment of a story from a Greek bestiary, or Book of Animals, in which a serpent poisons a waterhole and a unicorn purifies it.*

There are many old stories about unicorns purifying waterholes, ponds, lakes, wells. The Greek story was meant to be a religious parable, the horn standing for the Holy Cross, the serpent for the Devil, the poisoned pond for the sins of the world. But coming from a much later period, I read the story as a political fable and have retold it in my own way, with the unicorn as a kind of Gandhi figure.

The Unicorn and the Pool

It was evening at the pool, and the animals gathered to drink. It was the only time of day they did not fight or feed on one another.

This dusk, there was a strange oily substance floating on the water.

"What is this befouling our pool?" growled Lion. "Monkey, did you put it there?"

"Not I," said Monkey. He crept closer and touched the water tentatively. The substance moved away from his finger, then slid back, fouling his hand.

"Venom," Monkey said. He knew this sort of thing. "Monkeys do not have venom."

"Nor do buffalo," said Buffalo.

"Or giraffes," said Giraffe.

Hyena only giggled, but they knew he was not capable of any deceit, being open about his cravenness.

"Snake has done it," Lion said at last. And the others knew this was true, not because Lion said it, but because Snake had done the same thing many times before.

"We dare not drink now," Monkey added. And this, too, the animals knew.

Just then, as the last light of the sun sank behind the mountains, Unicorn came stepping across the veldt. Monkey, Buffalo, Giraffe, and Hyena gave way to him. Even Lion bowed his head, though just a little, as one king to another.

Unicorn's eyes were cloudy; his skin was yellow with age. Still he moved with grace. He stopped at the water's edge and stared, then bent his head toward the pond.

At the last moment, Monkey cried out: "O King of Kings, do not drink or you will die."

Unicorn hesitated but a moment, then dipped his horn into the pool.

Where the horn touched, the poison turned a bright blue, as if reflecting a pure cloudless sky. Then, in a moment, it darkened as if night had fallen, and was gone.

"Now you may drink, my children," Unicorn said. If anything, his eyes were cloudier than before. He turned and left the pool slowly, as if his bones ached, and where he stepped, flowers sprang up in his hoofprints.

All the animals thought they would see him again—all, that is, but Monkey. Gathering flowers, the red with the gold, Monkey made a crown of them. Days later, when the flowers wilted, Monkey wept. He wept not for the crown of flowers, nor for Unicorn, but for all of them who would soon have no proof against Snake's poison or their own bitter hearts.

The Elizabethan traveler Edward Webbe wrote, "I have seen in a place like a Park ajoying unto prester Iohn's Court, three score and seven-teene unicornes and eliphants all alive at one time, and they were so tame that I have played with them as one would play with young Lambes." This account, published in London in 1590 in a book called Edward Webbe: His Travailes, *is not to be trusted entirely.*

I borrowed the gates of ivory and horn—the gates of dreams—from Homer's Odyssey in order to make Webbe's account even more surely a matter of dream weaving.

A Visitor's Account

We went through the poison-proof gates,
one of ivory, one of horn,
and into the palace of Prester John:
the roof of pearly slates;
the doors nine kinds of wood
cunningly worked as if woven on looms;
rooms unfolding onto rooms,
and one especially set aside for the god
of the Abyssinians, whatever shape
he was that day to take.
We walked by an unrufflable lake,
the wind so cold, I wore a cape
lent by a guard, it richly sewn
as a king or emperor might wear it.
Yet the soldier undertook to share it,
indeed, would have given it me. "A loan,"
I insisted, handing it back

when we were in the palace once again.
And then I saw, tossing its mane,
a figure in silver outlined against black.
Your Royal Highness, I do not tell a lie.
In the park adjoining the court,
threescore and seventeen unicorns at sport,
horn to horn, so tame that I,

I strode among them with neither panic nor fear,
who would do no such thing amongst a herd of deer.

   (Signed) Edward Webbe

In Shepard's Lore of the Unicorn *there is a description of a walking stick made from unicorn horn and a reproduction of a London quack's advertisement, both of which I have made liberal use of in the making of this story.*

Heidi, Adam, and Jason are the names of my three children. They are all grown up now, Jason a photographer, Adam a musician, Heidi a private detective. This is not meant to be a portrait of any of them, though the age differences between them are correct.

But they love our Scottish house as much as I do, and so I thought it might amuse them to be put in a story that takes place there.

I am not Scottish. My father's people came from near Kiev, my mother's people from Latvia. But my husband is part Scottish, of the Douglas clan. We have loved Scotland ever since our first visit there, in the early 1980s, when we walked the Highland hills, strolled by misty dark lochs, and explored the stone brochs and the standing stones on Orkney.

There is, as the ward sister (nurse) implies in this story, still much magic left there.

The Healing Horn

It was Jason who found the walking stick, up in the attic of the Scottish house Great-grandmother Douglas had left them in her will. The stick was a long, straight wand of ivory that tapered to a blunt point and spiraled around to the end, as if someone had taken a smooth horn and carefully wrung it like a wet towel.

"What do you think it is?" Jason asked.

His sister, Heidi, shook her head. "I don't know. Just an old walking stick," she said. "Only a real fancy one."

But Adam, who was between Jason and Heidi in age and between them in temperament as well, said, "It's a unicorn horn."

"Sure," Heidi said. "Except a unicorn is a mythical beast."

"How do you know it's a unicorn horn?" Jason asked. "How do you know it's from a mythical beast?" He was always ready to believe either one of them if they gave him proper proof.

Heidi snorted and rolled her eyes. "*Everyone* knows unicorns are mythical beasts. Like dragons. Like Santa's reindeer." She was on safe ground, Jason having just that year finally given up his belief in Santa.

"Because of this!" Adam said triumphantly, holding up a tattered piece of yellowed paper. The paper was so old it was falling apart. "It was in the trunk next to the walking stick and they both have some string attached, as if they belong together." He began to read the paper out loud, "'UNICORNS HORN.'" He looked up and added, "It's an advertisement."

"Advert," Heidi said, looking over his shoulder. "It's called an advert over here. And someone doesn't know his punctuation." She was unhappy that Adam should have found the thing first. "There's an apostrophe missing. Besides, the unicorn is a mythical—"

"—beast," Adam finished for her. "Yes, so you said. But listen to this." He began reading the rest of the paper. "'Now brought in Ufe for the Cure of Difeafes by an Experienced DOCTOR, the AUTHOR of this Antidote.'"

"Someone doesn't know how to spell either," Heidi said. "Or use capitals." She read the paper over Adam's shoulder. "See, 'Ufe' should be 'use.'"

Adam nodded in sudden understanding. "So 'Difeafes' is really 'diseases.'"

Heidi continued, reading aloud now. "'A Moft . . . most . . . Excellent Drink made with a true Unicorns Horn, which doth Effectually

Cure these Diseases." She all but tore the paper out of Adam's hand in her eagerness. "Look at all those diseases: scurvy, ulcers, dropsie, running gout. . . ."

"They sound awful." Jason sat down on a Victorian sofa that was at once soft from its velvet covering and prickly from its horsehair padding. "Do we know what all those are?"

"No," Heidi said.

"Yes," Adam said at the same instant. "At least scurvy and ulcers."

"There's more," Heidi interrupted him. "'Consumption, Distillation, Coughs . . .'"

"I know coughs," Jason said.

"'Palpitations of the Heart,'" Heidi added. "'Fainting fits.'"

"Those, too," Jason said.

"You could cure an entire hospital," Adam put in.

Jason clutched the stick to his chest. "Wow!"

"'Convulsions, Kings Evil, Rickets in Children, Melancholy or sadness, the Green Sickness, and Obstructions,'" Heidi finished in a rush.

"You forgot one," Adam said. "'And all Distempers proceeding from a Cold Caufe.'"

"That's 'Cause.'" Heidi smiled when Adam looked miffed. She loved being able to correct him, which didn't happen very often.

Adam put the paper back in the trunk.

"What if it's true?" asked Jason. "We'd be rich." His voice quivered a bit. Being rich was a recent concern of theirs, ever since their father's business had gone broke. They'd taken the last of their savings to come over to Scotland to live in the big old house Great-grandmother Douglas had left them in St. Andrews. It was a place, their father said, where they could make a new start.

"Not only rich, but we'd be able to help the world, too," Heidi said. "Only, of course, it's not really true."

"Why not?" Jason's voice shook just a little.

"Because a unicorn," Heidi said, "really *is* just a mythical beast. And because that stick is probably just an antelope's horn."

"No antelopes in Scotland," Adam pointed out.

"Then a narwhale's horn. Or something." Heidi was adamant.

"What about the paper and what it said?" Jason asked.

Heidi turned away and stared at the ceiling, addressing it—a trick she had learned from her father. "Oh, *please*," she said. "It's an advertisement."

"Advert," Adam said.

"But," Jason said, and the excitement was high in his face, "but you have to tell the truth in advertising. Dad says it's the law!"

Heidi looked back at him pityingly. "It may be the law in America. But this is Scotland. We drive on the wrong side of the street here and, for all I know, advertise on the wrong side of the law. Besides, that paper is hundreds of years old and the law about truth in advertising isn't."

"How do *you* know?" wailed Jason, wanting the horn and the ad both to be true.

"We studied it in school," Heidi said.

This made Adam roll *his* eyes to the ceiling, but it was the only argument that would convince them. Heidi was two years older than Adam and four years older than Jason, which meant that she really *did* get to study things they never had even heard of. And she frequently reminded them of that.

St. Andrews was a city in Fife, which was a kind of state, except—as Mom pointed out—Fife was technically a kingdom. They all loved the idea of living in a kingdom—with a castle at one end of the street, near the ocean.

91

Great-grandmother Douglas's house had not one but two attics in which they were finding masses of odd and wonderful things, like a teapot with *MacKenzies Brothers* stamped on it, and dishes with gold rims, and inkwells and leather shoes that laced up to the knee and a moth-eaten blue-and-green kilt, and a silver stirrup cup. The attics were piled high with boxes and bags and trunks and it was going to take them weeks to sort through everything. Enough even—Mom had said—to start their own antique store, but Dad had vetoed that idea.

Mom and Dad had begun work on the attic with the good furniture in it and left the attic with the odds and ends for the children to explore. And that's how they'd come upon the trunk with the unicorn stick and the advert.

It was summer but not particularly hot in the attic, especially after they got the little round window open.

"Scotland never gets *particularly* hot," Dad had told them all, and he knew about this part of Scotland, having gone to the university a year while living in Great-grandmother Douglas's house. But it was hot enough, and dusty. There were frequent trips downstairs to make lemonade—with real lemons and lots of sugar.

"So," Jason said, "what do we tell Mom and Dad about the unicorn horn? And the diseases?"

"Nothing!" Adam and Heidi declared together. It was almost the only thing they agreed upon that morning. And so the secret was begun, over a pitcher of freshly made lemonade and a plate of buttered scones.

They spent the rest of the morning opening and closing the sixteen other large chests and the old wardrobe, but nothing they found engaged them like the horn and the advert. So at lunchtime, without

even discussing it, they packed a picnic and went off to the Dell, as they had christened the meadow playground at the far end of Ladebraes, the bird sanctuary behind their house. That far away, they couldn't be surprised by Mom or Dad or even short, stout Mr. Waring, the gardener. (Of course they could always count on him clearing and reclearing his throat, anyway, as an early warning signal. "Em . . ." he would say, and cough up something. "Em, younguns, what wee . . . em . . . delight are you . . . em . . . considerrrrrrring today?" He rolled his *rrr*s alarmingly. Jason was afraid one day Mr. Waring would get stuck, like a train on a siding, in a great rolling "rrrrrrrr . . ." and they would have to poke him to get him started again.)

In the Dell, surrounded by Autumn crocuses, sweetly purple against the grass, Heidi made a proposal.

"Not that I believe it, of course," she said, "but we need to research unicorns. Maybe there's *some* truth . . ."

She and Jason looked pointedly at Adam. He was the family's great reader. Clearly, research was his strong point.

"All right," he said, as if reluctant, but actually that was all show. He couldn't wait to get to the library. It meant riding his bike down to the center of town and really exploring the library stacks, something he hadn't yet done properly. At least, not *properly* as he meant it, without being pulled out by Jason's or Heidi's quick choices. "All right," he said. "But only if I can do it alone."

"Of course," Heidi said. "Jason is going to find out more about advertising from Dad, and I—"

"How do I do that?" Jason wailed. At eight, and still painfully shy, he found this a daunting proposition, even if it was only Dad he had to tackle.

"And I will find out about diseases," Heidi went on imperturbably.

"You hate libraries," Adam pointed out.

"I will be at the doctor's office," Heidi said. "Because I shall be Terribly Ill and Need To See Specialists." She put her hand to her forehead and pretended to swoon. Acting was her one great specialty.

"That will cost money," Jason pointed out. His forehead was creased with worry. "And we don't have any."

"Not in Scotland," Heidi said knowingly. "Here they have social-ized medicine."

"What's that?" Jason asked.

"Free," Adam said. "Their medicine doesn't cost them anything."

"Oh." Jason didn't really understand at first what that meant, and then, in one of those great intuitive leaps of understanding he some-times made that proved him miles ahead of his brother and sister, he said, "But if it's free, then how are we going to ever make money from selling the unicorn medicine?"

"That's not the point of this," Heidi said.

But Adam smiled. "TV and book rights," he said.

This answer satisfied Jason and there were no more hard questions after that.

It didn't go exactly as planned.

Adam started out well enough in the library but got sidetracked by a book on mythical beasts and spent a whole day reading about Scottish creatures like nuggles and boggarts and kelpies.

Jason tried to engage his father in a conversation about advertising but instead got a long lecture on not believing everything he read or heard.

And Heidi—after three hours in the doctor's waiting room ("I now understand why it's called that!" her mother said in exasperation)—was pronounced fit, except for a sore throat that she had produced herself by faking a cough. "Fisherman's Friend" was what the doctor advised, and that turned out to be the world's most horrible-tasting lozenge, which her mother insisted she had to suck on.

"*I* deserve a medal!" Heidi moaned when the three were once again in the attic. It was misting out, with some rain, what the Scots called a *haar*, and Mom would not let them outside. "I have never tasted anything so awful in my life."

"Try using the stick against your throat, then," Jason suggested.

Only half believing, Heidi took the walking stick and held it, gingerly, against her throat.

Nothing happened.

"Well, of course nothing is going to happen that way," Adam said. "It's got to be ground up in a drink. At least that's what the advert says."

"And drunk?" Heidi was aghast. Her throat suddenly felt better. When she told them so, Jason smiled.

"See," he said.

They couldn't convince him that it was the threat of using the ground-up horn, not the horn itself, that had cured Heidi. They went to bed that night with Jason still convinced—as only an eight-year-old can be—that the unicorn horn had worked as per the advertisement.

In the morning—and it got to be morning at four-thirty, with birds shouting into the light—Jason was still sure of it. He padded into Heidi's room and sat on her bed.

"We *will* make our fortunes," he said. "And Mom and Dad will be happy again."

Adam heard them talking and came in as well. "Not much of a fortune with only one horn. Once it's ground up, it's gone."

"But we don't have to grind it up," Jason said. "It cured Heidi by—"

"I AM NOT CURED!" Heidi shouted. Then, remembering that her parents were still asleep in the bedroom down the hall, she whispered, "I am *not* cured."

"Are, too," Jason pointed out sensibly. "Otherwise you couldn't shout."

"I . . . was . . . never . . . really . . . sick," Heidi said carefully. "I was acting. To find out about medicine here." She stomped out of the room, whispering fiercely back over her shoulder at Adam, "I give up."

She could hear Adam explaining, as she started down the stairs, "A scientist would never take just one cure as proof." She thought fiercely, *Bad idea, Adam.*

It was.

By that afternoon Jason—who had been much too shy in the States to make many friends—was outside their house on the sidewalk, stopping strangers and asking if they were sick. Most of the Scots he stopped thought his accent charming and asked where he was from. But not one of them would admit to being ill.

So Jason went down the path through the bird sanctuary and came back three hours later, his backpack laden with dying animals: a wood pigeon, a thrush, and a hedgehog less sick than terrified. He put them in makeshift cages made of packing crates. Next he knocked off the tip of the walking stick with a hammer and ground it to pieces. Taking some of his great-grandmother's Madeira—she had left quite a collection of wines and whiskeys—he mixed in the grainy residue.

Then, with a cloth dipped in the solution, he dripped his home-made medicine into the beaks of the two birds and, rather more carefully, onto the hedgehog's nose.

Within the hour the birds flew off drunkenly and the hedgehog fell asleep, too full of wine to keep trembling.

"I think he will be fine in the morning," Jason announced triumphantly to Adam and Heidi.

"I think he will have a hangover in the morning," Heidi said disgustedly, looking up at the lowering sky.

"What makes you think it is a he?" Adam asked.

In the morning the hedgehog was gone, the box mysteriously tipped over. Heidi suspected the neighbor's marmalade cat, but she didn't say this to Jason. Anyway, he was too full of himself to care.

"I did it! I did it!" he crowed. "Let's tell Mom and Dad."

"Let's not," Heidi cautioned. "You know how they can be."

"Besides," Adam added, "they are much too busy right now."

Since it was rare that the two of them agreed on anything, Jason caved in. But he headed down Ladebraes and through the sanctuary for another sick-animal reconnaissance.

"I don't like this," Heidi said, watching him go.

"It's not like home, in the States," Adam reminded her. "We are allowed to go off alone here. It's safer. Dad says so."

"Right," Heidi agreed.

But they were both wrong.

Three hours later there was a phone call, and suddenly the household was full of frantic activity. Jason had climbed a tree after a nestful of birds. He had fallen, rolling down the hill and into Kinness Burn, the little stream that wound through the braes. Found by a local man who was out walking a dog, Jason had been crying for his mother. An ambulance had taken him to hospital, but it was three hours before he could remember his proper address. Concussions can do that. And new addresses.

The local policeman had come knocking on their door.

Everyone hurried into the car. Twice Dad forgot which side of the road to drive on, and they were almost in an accident with a big lorry. But finally they made it to the hospital.

Jason was in a ward with three other children, looking pleased with himself though white as the bed sheet. A ward nurse was sitting by his side, talking to him. She was a terrifyingly big woman, with shoulders—Dad said later—like a linebacker. But she was wonderfully soft-spoken.

"Here's Mummy and Daddy now," she said, smiling. "Now don't you go and frighten them further, there's a good lad."

Jason smiled up at them. "Did you bring it?" he asked.

"Bring what?" Mom looked both puzzled and relieved.

"No," Heidi said. "It's nonsense."

"I *need* it," Jason said. "For my cure."

"Bring what?" Dad asked rather dangerously, talking to the ceiling. Then he turned to Adam and looked directly at him. "Bring what?"

"A walking stick," Adam said.

Heidi broke in. "He's got this bizarro idea that the stick is a uni-corn horn and that it can cure things."

"Animals," said Adam.

"People, too," Jason said. His face was still pearly white but there were two spots of color, one on each cheek. "Don't you remember? I'm the one with the concussion, and I remember. Ulcers and coughs and scurvies."

"Do you mean scurvy, dear?" the ward sister asked. "We don't get much of that nowadays."

"And gout," Jason said.

"You won't have that at your age." The ward sister's face was quite serious. "Besides, I think a concussion is dire enough."

"But it cures *everything*," Jason wailed. "And I *need* it."

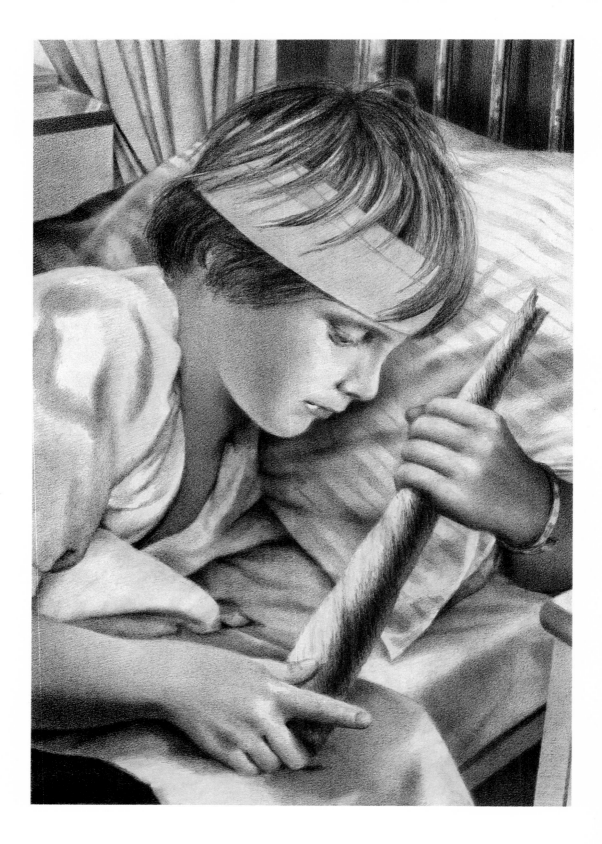

"Don't be . . ." Dad began.

" . . . silly," Mom finished.

But the ward sister stood and put her hand up. "If the boy thinks it will help," she said, "it will. This is"—and she smiled at them—"a country of much magic." Then she bustled crisply out of the room.

They rescued the stick from the back garden.

"This is it?" Dad asked.

They nodded.

"But it's . . . it's . . ." Mom said.

"Broken," Heidi explained. "Just the tip. He ground it up. In Great-grandmother Douglas's wine."

"*No wine!*" Dad said to the sky.

They nodded.

"It's a horrible old thing," Mom said as they got back into the car and returned—carefully on the left side of the road—to the hospital.

The stick was presented to Jason with a great flourish. He put both hands on it and color flooded back to his face.

"I feel lots better now," he said to the ward sister.

"That's a good lad," she said. "But just in case, we will keep you overnight. Sometimes these old sticks don't have enough juice left for more than half a healing. You can keep it by your side, though."

"I think I'll lend it to Ronnie," he said. "He needs it more than me."

The ward nurse walked the family outside. "He's a tough little laddie," she said. "And no real broken bones. But Doctor wants him to stay for observation."

"Who is Ronnie?" Mom asked.

"Oh, he's the laddie with liver problems. He's in once a week for dialysis. Your Jason and he have become great friends. It's good for them both."

Mom and Dad went to consult with the doctor, but Heidi and Adam stayed with the ward sister.

"The stick . . . ?" Heidi asked.

"Will it help?" finished Adam.

She looked at them both and smiled. "It certainly canna hurt," she said slowly. "With magic things, that's the best we can ask for. But we can always *hope* for more."

They went back to the house and returned to the attic.

"Do you think there might be more?" Adam asked.

"More sticks?"

"More magic."

Heidi smiled. "Well," she said, "it *is* Scotland, after all. As the nurse said."

"Said what?" He looked puzzled. Heidi loved when that happened.

"It canna hurt. And—we can *always* hope for more."

I wrote this poem in college. It was published in the Grecourt Review, *the college literary magazine, and won me a following. It also contributed to my winning all the poetry prizes my senior year, and helped get me into the Poetry Society of America. (Though two years later, when I was engaged, the* New York Times *insisted I was in the Pottery Society of America, which probably led to a confusion that has lasted until this day among bibliographers.)*

I look back at some of my early writing with a mixture of amusement and despair. Some—like this poem—I still like. Much of it, though, seems to me incredibly amateurish or at least unformed. Or uninformed. The thing about being a writer is that one has a chance to get better. We revise not only our stories but, in a sense, our abilities, our lives. Unlike professions like sports or art forms like dance, writing is the kind of work where you can grow older and grow up into your potential.

At least I hope that is what is happening with me.

Rhinoceros

Bloated relic of a past
Where hungry behemoths
In ponderous herds lumbered
Through the swamp-swilled woods:
Behind the folds of unwashed poundage,
Behind that muted horn of plenty,
Pink eyes, myopic and small,
Strain into the African muds.

Preposterous nose,
Elephantine toes,

Cyclopean rear,
Cumbrous ear,
Down to a wee-wispish,
Barely switch-tipped
Tail.

And yet the memory of a swift
And silken racer of the wind,
Golden horn rippling the pool
Of dreams, troubles my mind.
What alchemy of the last few worlds,
What lava-filled abyss
Transformed that silken fair?
Has the unicorn come to this?

I first came upon the k'i-lin (or ki-lin) in Jorge Luis Borges's Book of Imaginary Beings. I found a much fuller exploration of the Chinese unicorn in Shepard's Lore of the Unicorn. Borges used much of the same wording, so I knew where he had done his research! However, though I borrowed some Chinese "facts," the story I am telling is not really Chinese at all. The ideas are purely Western.

I wrote the beginning of this story about three weeks before the ending came to me. I had reached the part where I had put down, "But what he didn't know was why it was in his henyard." And I said aloud to my typewriter, "I don't know why, either." (This was not a joke. I really hadn't a clue.)

There the story sat while I did a lot of other things: took a trip to a friend's house by train, a trip that took seven hours; got the car serviced; read three books; wrote innumerable letters; composed two new poems; went to lunch and dinner with neighbors. Anything, in fact, but dealing with why the unicorn was in Li Po's henyard.

And then, the day before I was to go back home from Scotland, the very day the rental service was coming to take away the rented typewriter, I sat down and out it came: the visit to the sage, the prophecy, and all the rest.

So there you have the writing process in a nutshell. For me, at least, it has less to do with thinking than with neglecting. Sometimes if I don't think about a story, it solves itself. Or resolves itself.

Li Po and the Unicorn

Li Po heard a squawking among his chickens. It was a high squawking, wild and furious.

Fox in the yard, he thought. He had been greatly troubled with them of late. Grabbing his stick, he limped around the corner and came face to face not with the expected fox but with a beast he had never seen before. It had the body of a deer, the tail of an ox, and the hooves of a horse.

"What can this be?" he asked aloud, holding the stick in front of him, for the animal had a short horn stuck right in the middle of its forehead. However, Li Po soon saw that it was not a fearsome horn at all, the tip being made of flesh rather than ivory. So he lowered the stick, but only a little bit.

Looking more closely at the beast, Li Po also saw that its coat was of five mixed colors—except for the belly, which was a yellow-brown, like dirt in the garden when it has been too long without rain.

Suddenly the animal opened its mouth and a strange cry like the ringing of a bell issued from its throat.

That was when Li Po knew that it was a *k'i-lin*, a unicorn. He breathed a sigh, of relief really, and put the stick down, for to wound a k'i-lin is extremely unlucky and Li Po already had enough bad luck: a fox among his hens, too little water for his garden, and money owing the factor for his house and land.

"Perhaps you are an omen for good," he said to the k'i-lin, "like the dragon and the phoenix and the tortoise, though I have never seen the first two at all, and the third only once, and it on the very day I met my wife." And thinking of his wife, dead now a year, Li Po sighed. They had planned for a long and happy life together, but she had died giving birth to their child. He had buried them both behind the house, where he visited them every day.

The k'i-lin said nothing.

"Or perhaps," Li Po continued, a year alone having made him at ease talking to himself, "perhaps you are a sign that I am getting old and will soon join my dear wife and child." But he did not believe that. Except for a limp that he had had forever, on account of falling from his horse as a soldier, his health was excellent and he was still a young man.

"Or else I am going mad." But that, he knew, was not a possible answer at all. Li Po, whatever his other attributes, had never been cursed with an imagination. As a soldier and now as a farmer, he knew only what *was*. He never thought about what *could be* or what *might be*. "Do not borrow trouble" was what he had always cautioned his wife.

So then Li Po knew that the animal before him was, indeed, a k'i-lin, one of the four animals of Good Omen whose life span is one thousand years and who come down from Heaven now and again to mix with the people. But what he didn't know was why it was in his henyard.

After giving the creature a mixture of rice and sour milk—he knew well enough it would not eat anything alive, not even live grass—Li Po enclosed it gently in his barn, quartering it next to Mist Over Mountain, his recalcitrant mule. Then he went at once to the house of Lao Chang, the scholar priest who lived on the outskirts of the village.

Lao Chang spoke only once every two weeks. The rest of his time was spent in contemplation. Li Po did not know whether the appointed day for speaking was at hand, for he had never gone for a consultation, but at least—so he thought—he could pose questions. Lao Chang listened, even when he did not speak.

Li Po brought a bottle of his best wine as a thanks offering and set it down on the sage's doorstep. Then he went to the window, which was drawn open just a bit. Squatting on his haunches, Li Po poured out the tale of his discovery.

"O Master of Answers," Li Po began, for it is always best to flatter a sage before asking for help, "in my henyard just now I have come upon a k'i-lin. The reason I know is that there is a fleshy horn in the center of its forehead, a coat of five mixed colors on its back. And when it opened its mouth, it sang out with a strange cry like a bell. But I do not know why such a creature is in my henyard. Can you enlighten me?"

Li Po was actually expecting nothing but silence in return for his question, but either the question was of great interest to the sage or this was, fortuitously, his day to speak. There came from behind the window a powerful clearing of the throat, and then an old man's voice, thready and weak, addressed Li Po.

"A goat may have such a horn, my son. A horse may have such a coat. But no creature saving the blessed k'i-lin makes such a noise. If it has deigned to come into your henyard, it is to bring you something of great import."

"I had hoped, Master of Information," said Li Po, "that it would bring me some luck. I could use some."

"What is luck?" asked the sage. "Is it luck to join the gaming table and gather in many coins, or luckier still to know just when to leave?"

Li Po did not answer.

"Is it luck to be born a prince and then to lose one's head in a revolution, or luckier still to be a peasant tilling the fields during a long and healthy life?"

Li Po could not answer.

"Is it luck," the sage went on, "to have met and married the perfect wife who dies too young, or luckier still never to have married at all and saved yourself the agony?"

This Li Po might have answered, but yet he was silent.

The sage chuckled, a sound like wind over dry reeds. Li Po was glad, then, that he had made no attempt to answer, for *no* answer was the correct one.

The sage said, "Luck—what is it? Neither the wise man nor the fool knows for sure."

109

Li Po waited for a minute, hoping to understand all that the sage had told him. Or hoping that more of an answer would be forthcoming. But the window was drawn closed; clearly the sage was through speaking.

No more enlightened than before, Li Po stood and went home.

The henyard was silent, although—Li Po counted quickly—the hens were all alive and well. He went into the barn and there was the k'i-lin, sleeping. As it slept, it made again the sound of a bell, though this time the sound came through its nose.

Li Po reached out a hand to it, then drew back. *It has come so far, it must be tired, poor thing*, he thought. *I shall not disturb its rest.* He went around his small holding on tiptoe, so as not to make any loud sounds. He fed the hens, but quietly. He built up his fire and boiled water for tea, but quietly. He did not chat companionably to himself, nor did he sing, though he did miss the sound.

His wife had had a lovely voice and when he thought of her, which was never less than three or four times a day, it was that voice he missed most of all.

When the k'i-lin woke, Li Po gave it some more rice and milk, not so sour this time, and he brushed its silky mane with his wife's old comb, the only thing he could think of that would suit that delicate hair. All the while, he waited patiently—a farmer and a soldier both learn a good deal of patience—for the k'i-lin to give him the thing of great import. *A message*, he thought. *Or a pot of gold*, he thought. *Or a message about a pot of gold*, he hoped.

But the k'i-lin did not speak.

A second day went by, the sky the color of candle wax. And a third, with a storm foreshortening the landscape and turning over all the leaves. Still, the k'i-lin told him nothing of import. He mentioned it to his wife at her grave.

Li Po went back to the sage's house, armed with a second bottle of wine, not so good as the first. He positioned himself by the window, squatting again on his heels. But when he asked his question, "Why is the k'i-lin in my barn and why has it given me no message?," the sage did not reply.

So Li Po went home to a desultory supper of rice and steamed greens. He drank no wine. All that was left was a bad vintage. His good bottles had gotten him nothing in return.

A lesser man might have screamed at the k'i-lin, demanding some sign. Or turned the k'i-lin out of doors. But somehow Li Po felt sorry for it. He gave up hope of any recompense but fed it as he would any of his animals, and combed its delicate hair with the same patience with which he had combed his dying wife's hair.

If this comforted the k'i-lin, it did not indicate that to Li Po, even by as much as a flicker of an eyelid. If it noticed him, it did not show it by even so much as a shrug of its shoulder. It ate, it drank, it slept.

But speaking to it, Li Po felt, somehow, content.

The three days went by, then three more, and a week, ten days, two weeks. Li Po took his last bottle of wine and went off to see the sage. This day there was a line of waiting villagers. By the time it was Li Po's turn, the window was shut.

Li Po went home, drinking the vinegary wine as he went. It did not suit his stomach and so, tired and short of temper, he went out into the barn.

Mist Over Mountain, the mule, stared at him. But the k'i-lin was gone.

Nothing even remained to show that the creature had been there for fourteen days, eating Li Po's food, except for a small bundle of rags in the hay. Li Po touched it with his foot, ready to let the anger he was feeling flare into a raging fire, when the rags cried out. All temper left Li Po then, and he knelt down.

There, staring up at him, was a child with eyes as yellow-brown as the k'i-lin's belly hair, as yellow-brown as dirt in a garden too long without rain.

Li Po picked the child up, saying, "I have no son of my own, so I shall raise you myself." But he needed advice, never having held a live child in his arms.

So he ran back to the sage's house and did not wait patiently at the window. He went directly to the door and hammered on it loudly. When no one answered, he walked right in.

The sage looked up from his tea. "Ah," he said, "the farmer who would have luck. Did you know the k'i-lin comes in the shape of an incomparable man, a revealer of mysteries to all humankind?"

"He has come," the farmer said sharply, "as a baby."

"Just so," said the sage, "and if you follow your heart, you will raise him well. When the child is old enough, bring him to me and I shall teach him wisdom." Then he turned back to his tea.

But when the child was old enough for teaching, he already was wise in the ways of plums ripening on the bough, the ways of bees dancing before the hive, the ways of worms eating along the mulberry leaves, the ways of light glancing off the water, and the sound of dry earth sucking at rain. He was a farmer's son, and so his wisdom was in its own way greater than that of the old sage.

Besides, the boy had a voice that rang like a bell and he sang all the day long, which was a pleasure to Li Po and a reminder of the child's dead mother. (For Li Po had made himself forget that the child was not his own.)

So the boy stayed at home, a comfort to his father in his old age. He married a village woman and they surrounded Li Po with grandchildren who loved to listen to his stories. One of those grandchildren became an incomparable man, a great leader who ruled his people wisely.

Who is to say what is luck? Or what it has to do with love? Or—for that matter—with wisdom?

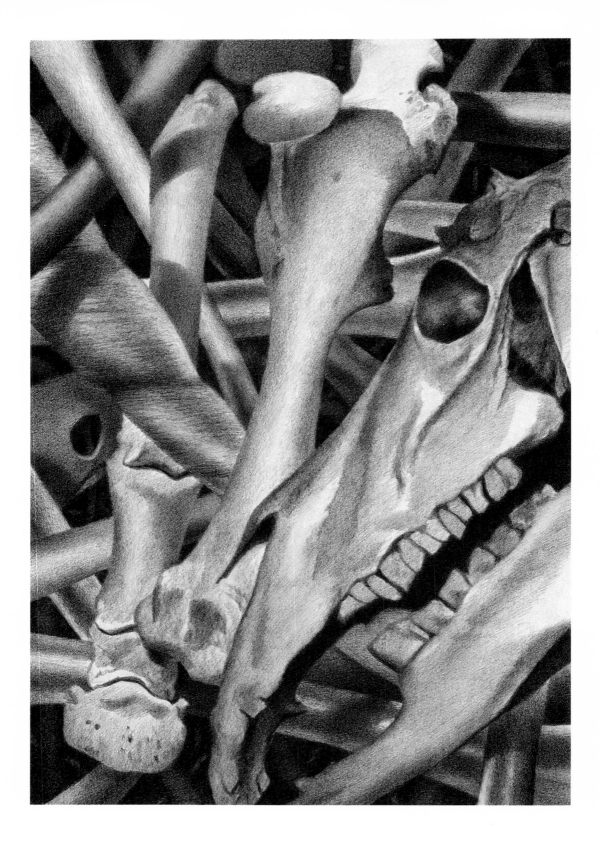

On a lovely Fall day, when I should have been out enjoying the sunshine, birding with my husband, I found myself up in the Aerie, my attic writing room in my Massachusetts home, writing this poem. It is based on the very dubious fossil discoveries of the sixteenth and seventeenth centuries in China—of dragon bones—and in Quedlinberg, Germany—of unicorn bones. Even though people did not altogether accept the idea these were the bones of mythical animals, they still enjoyed believing in the myths.

As do I—or I wouldn't be writing all these stories and poems.

Fossils

We excavated dragon bones
from the layered beds
of Chinese rocks:
great femurs strong enough
to stand a saurus.
But the lighter bones,
with a browbone thick as a shin,
we did not find till Quedlinberg,
in a cave covered with sign.

Does it matter no one believes us,
rejecting the substance,
accepting the shadow?